W9-CKI-392

# Dazzling cookies

Publications International, Ltd.

Favorite Brand Name Recipes at www.fbnr.com

**Copyright © 2009 Publications International, Ltd.**
All rights reserved. This publication may not be reproduced or quoted in whole or in part by any means whatsoever without written permission from:

Louis Weber, CEO
Publications International, Ltd.
7373 North Cicero Avenue
Lincolnwood, IL 60712

Permission is never granted for commercial purposes.

All recipes and photographs that contain specific brand names are copyrighted by those companies and/or associations, unless otherwise specified. All photographs *except* those on pages 115 and 124 copyright © Publications International, Ltd.

DOLE® is a registered trademark of Dole Food Company, Inc.

™/© M&M's, M and the M&M's Characters are trademarks of Mars, Incorporated.
© Mars, Inc. 2009.

Nestlé and Toll House are registered trademarks of Nestlé.

Some of the products listed in this publication may be in limited distribution.

**Pictured on the front cover:** Original Nestlé® Toll House® Chocolate Chip Cookies *(page 72)*.
**Pictured on the back cover** *(left to right):* Basic Oatmeal Cookies *(page 149)* and Butterscotch Toffee Gingersnap Squares *(page 24)*.

ISBN-13: 978-1-4127-9789-4
ISBN-10: 1-4127-9789-6

Library of Congress Control Number: 2009920599

Manufactured in China.

8 7 6 5 4 3 2 1

**Microwave Cooking:** Microwave ovens vary in wattage. Use the cooking times as guidelines and check for doneness before adding more time.

**Preparation/Cooking Times:** Preparation times are based on the approximate amount of time required to assemble the recipe before cooking, baking, chilling or serving. These times include preparation steps such as measuring, chopping and mixing. The fact that some preparations and cooking can be done simultaneously is taken into account. Preparation of optional ingredients and serving suggestions is not included.

# table of contents

classic goodies . . . . . . . . . . . . . . . . . . . . . . . 4

global flavors . . . . . . . . . . . . . . . . . . . . . . . 28

chocolate obsession . . . . . . . . . . . . . . . . . . . 52

fruit fantasy . . . . . . . . . . . . . . . . . . . . . . . 76

kids' favorites . . . . . . . . . . . . . . . . . . . . . . 102

seasonal treats . . . . . . . . . . . . . . . . . . . . . 126

doughs & icings . . . . . . . . . . . . . . . . . . . . . 148

acknowledgments . . . . . . . . . . . . . . . . . . . . 155

index . . . . . . . . . . . . . . . . . . . . . . . . . . . . 156

# Classic goodies

## peanut butter toffee chewies

1 package (about 18 ounces) yellow cake mix
  with pudding in the mix

1 cup peanut butter

1/4 cup (1/2 stick) butter, softened

1/4 cup water

1 egg

1-1/3 cups milk chocolate toffee bits, divided

1. Preheat oven to 350°F. Line cookie sheets with parchment paper.

2. Beat cake mix, peanut butter, butter, water and egg in large bowl with electric mixer at medium speed 1 minute or until well blended. Stir in 1 cup toffee bits.

3. Drop dough by rounded teaspoonfuls about 1-1/2 inches apart on prepared cookie sheets. Flatten tops of cookies slightly with back of teaspoon. Sprinkle about 1/4 teaspoon reserved toffee bits into center of each cookie.

4. Bake 10 to 12 minutes or until edges are lightly browned. Cool 5 minutes on cookie sheets. Remove to wire racks; cool completely.

**Prep Time:** 15 minutes
**Bake Time:** 12 minutes

Makes
about 4 dozen
cookies

# oatmeal date bars

2 packages (18 ounces each) refrigerated oatmeal raisin cookie dough

2-1/2 cups uncooked old-fashioned oats, divided

2 packages (8 ounces each) chopped dates

1 cup water

1/2 cup sugar

1 teaspoon vanilla

1. Let dough stand at room temperature about 15 minutes. Preheat oven to 350°F. Lightly grease 13×9-inch baking pan.

2. Combine three fourths of one package of dough and 1 cup oats in medium bowl; beat until well blended. Set aside.

3. Combine remaining dough and 1-1/2 cups oats in large bowl; beat until well blended. Press dough evenly onto bottom of prepared pan. Bake 10 minutes.

4. Meanwhile, combine dates, water and sugar in medium saucepan; bring to a boil over high heat. Boil 3 minutes; remove from heat and stir in vanilla. Spread date mixture evenly over partially baked crust; sprinkle evenly with topping mixture.

5. Bake 25 to 28 minutes or until bubbly. Cool completely in pan on wire rack. Cut into bars.

Makes about
3 dozen bars

*Classic* **goodies**

# whoopie pies

1 package (about 18 ounces) devil's food cake mix without pudding in the mix

1 package (4-serving size) chocolate instant pudding and pie filling mix

1-1/4 cups (2-1/2 sticks) butter, softened, divided

4 eggs

1 cup water

1-1/4 cups marshmallow crème

3/4 cup powdered sugar

1/2 teaspoon vanilla

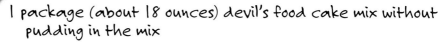

Makes 2 dozen sandwich cookies

1. Preheat oven to 350°F. Grease cookie sheets.

2. Beat cake mix, pudding mix, 1/2 cup (1 stick) butter, eggs and water in large bowl with electric mixer at low speed until moistened. Beat at medium speed 2 minutes or until light and thick, scraping down side of bowl frequently. Drop batter by heaping tablespoonfuls 2 inches apart on prepared cookie sheets.

3. Bake 12 to 14 minutes or until cookies spring back when lightly touched. Cool 5 minutes on cookie sheets. Remove to wire racks; cool completely.

4. Meanwhile, beat remaining 3/4 cup (1-1/2 sticks) butter, marshmallow crème, powdered sugar and vanilla in large bowl at high speed about 2 minutes or until light and fluffy.

5. Spread filling on flat side of half of cookies; top with remaining cookies.

# red velvet brownies

1 package (about 18 ounces) red velvet cake mix

3/4 cup (1-1/2 sticks) butter, softened

2 eggs

1-1/2 cups chopped pecans, divided

1 container (16 ounces) prepared cream cheese frosting

Red sprinkles (optional)

**Makes 3 dozen brownies**

1. Preheat oven 350°F. Line 13×9-inch baking pan with foil, leaving 1-inch overhang. Spray foil with nonstick cooking spray.

2. Beat cake mix, butter and eggs in large bowl with electric mixer at medium speed 1 minute. (Mixture will be thick.) Add 1 cup pecans; beat 15 seconds or just until combined. Spray fingers with cooking spray; gently spread batter evenly in prepared pan.

3. Bake 25 minutes or until toothpick inserted into center comes out almost clean. Cool completely in pan on wire rack.

4. Spread frosting over brownies; sprinkle with remaining 1/2 cup pecans and sprinkles, if desired. Refrigerate at least 2 hours before cutting. Store covered in refrigerator.

# gingersnaps

2-1/2 cups all-purpose flour

1-1/2 teaspoons ground ginger

1 teaspoon baking soda

1 teaspoon ground allspice

1/2 teaspoon salt

1-1/2 cups sugar

2 tablespoons margarine, softened

1/2 cup MOTT'S® Apple Sauce

1/4 cup GRANDMA'S® Molasses

**Makes 3 dozen cookies**

1. Preheat oven to 375°F. Spray cookie sheets with nonstick cooking spray.

2. In medium bowl, sift together flour, ginger, baking soda, allspice and salt.

3. In large bowl, beat sugar and margarine with electric mixer at medium speed until blended. Whisk in apple sauce and molasses.

4. Add flour mixture to apple sauce mixture; stir until well blended.

5. Drop rounded tablespoonfuls of dough 1 inch apart onto prepared cookie sheets. Flatten each slightly with moistened fingertips.

6. Bake 12 to 15 minutes or until firm. Cool completely on wire rack.

# chocolate and oat toffee bars

3/4 cup (1-1/2 sticks) plus 2 tablespoons butter, softened, divided

1 package (about 18 ounces) yellow cake mix with pudding in the mix

2 cups uncooked quick oats

1/4 cup packed brown sugar

1 egg

1/2 teaspoon vanilla

1 cup toffee baking bits

1/2 cup chopped pecans

1/3 cup semisweet chocolate chips

**Makes 3 dozen bars**

1. Preheat oven to 350°F. Grease 13×9-inch baking pan.

2. Beat 3/4 cup butter in large bowl with electric mixer at medium speed until creamy. Add cake mix, oats, brown sugar, egg and vanilla; beat 1 minute or until well blended. Stir in toffee bits and pecans. Press dough into prepared pan.

3. Bake 30 to 35 minutes or until golden brown. Cool completely in pan on wire rack.

4. Melt remaining 2 tablespoons butter and chocolate chips in small saucepan over low heat. Drizzle warm glaze over bars. Let stand at room temperature 1 hour or until glaze is set.

Unless a recipe otherwise states, always measure brown sugar by packing it firmly into a measuring cup.

# caramel-kissed pecan cookies

1 package (about 18 ounces) refrigerated sugar cookie dough

1/2 cup all-purpose flour

1 package (2 ounces) ground pecans

12 caramel-filled milk chocolate kiss candies, unwrapped

1 package (2 ounces) pecan chips

Caramel ice cream topping, warmed

1. Let dough stand at room temperature 15 minutes. Preheat oven 350°F. Line cookie sheet with parchment paper.

2. Beat dough, flour and ground pecans in medium bowl until well blended. Divide into 12 equal pieces. Place one chocolate candy in center of each piece of dough. Shape dough into ball around candies; seal well. Roll each ball in pecan chips. Place 2 inches apart on prepared cookie sheet.

3. Bake 16 to 18 minutes or until light golden around edges. Cool cookies 2 minutes on cookie sheet.

4. Drizzle caramel over warm cookies. Remove cookies to wire rack; cool completely. Store in airtight container.

Makes 1 dozen cookies

# classic layer bars

Store leftover coconut in an airtight container for up to 1 week in the refrigerator or up to 6 months in the freezer. Store leftover coconut in an airtight container for up to 1 week in the refrigerator in the freezer.

1-1/2 cups graham cracker crumbs

1/2 cup (1 stick) butter, melted

1-1/3 cups shredded coconut

1-1/2 cups semisweet chocolate chips or chunks*

1 cup chopped nuts

1 can (14 ounces) sweetened condensed milk

*You may substitute white chocolate, butterscotch or peanut butter chips for the chocolate chips.

1. Preheat oven to 350°F. Grease 13×9-inch baking pan. Combine graham cracker crumbs and butter in medium bowl; press firmly into prepared pan.

2. Sprinkle coconut, chocolate chips and nuts over crumb layer; press down firmly. Pour sweetened condensed milk evenly over top.

3. Bake 25 to 30 minutes or until golden brown. Cool completely in pan on wire rack. Cut into bars.

Note: Reduce oven temperature to 325°F if using a glass baking dish.

Makes about
3 dozen bars

# tea cookies

3 cups granulated sugar

2 cups shortening

2 teaspoons vanilla

4 eggs

5-1/2 cups all-purpose flour

4 teaspoons cream of tartar

2 teaspoons baking soda

1/2 teaspoon salt

1 cup finely chopped almonds, walnuts or pecans (optional)

Powdered sugar (optional)

Makes about 8 dozen cookies

1. Preheat oven to 375°F.

2. Beat granulated sugar, shortening and vanilla in large bowl with electric mixer at medium speed until creamy. Add eggs, one at a time, beating well after each addition. Continue beating until mixture is smooth.

3. Combine flour, cream of tartar, baking soda and salt in large bowl. Stir in nuts, if desired. Add sugar mixture; beat until well blended.

4. Shape dough into walnut-sized balls. Place 2 inches apart on ungreased cookie sheets. Bake 8 to 10 minutes or until lightly browned around edges.

# crispy toffee cookies

1/2 cup all-purpose flour

1/2 cup unsalted dry roasted
   peanuts

1/8 teaspoon salt

1/2 cup packed light brown sugar

1/3 cup butter

1/4 cup light corn syrup

1 teaspoon vanilla

Chocolate, melted

**Makes
about 4 dozen
cookies**

1. Preheat oven to 375°F. Line two cookie sheets with parchment paper.

2. Combine flour, peanuts and salt in food processor; process until mixture resembles coarse crumbs.

3. Combine brown sugar, butter and corn syrup in medium saucepan; bring to a boil over medium heat, stirring frequently. Remove from heat; stir in peanut mixture and vanilla until well blended. Return pan to low heat; keep warm. Spoon 6 rounded half teaspoonfuls of batter 3 inches apart on one prepared cookie sheet.

4. Bake exactly 4 minutes. While cookies are baking, spoon batter on second cookie sheet. When cookies have baked 4 minutes, immediately remove from oven. (Cookies will be very light and will appear not to be completely baked.) Slide parchment paper with cookies onto wire rack; cool completely. Drizzle cookies with melted chocolate.

5. While second batch of cookies is baking, line first cookie sheet of with new sheet of parchment paper; continue to prepare and bake cookies in batches of six. Peel cookies from parchment paper; store in airtight container with parchment paper between layers to prevent cookies from sticking.

# mississippi mud bars

3/4 cup packed brown sugar

1/2 cup (1 stick) butter, softened

1 egg

1 teaspoon vanilla

1/2 teaspoon baking soda

1/4 teaspoon salt

1 cup plus 2 tablespoons all-purpose flour

1 cup (6 ounces) semisweet chocolate chips, divided

1 cup (6 ounces) white chocolate chips, divided

1/2 cup chopped walnuts or pecans

Makes about 3 dozen bars

1. Preheat oven to 375°F. Line 9-inch square pan with foil; grease foil.

2. Beat brown sugar and butter in large bowl with electric mixer at medium speed until well blended. Beat in egg and vanilla until blended. Blend in baking soda and salt. Add flour; mix until well blended. Stir in 2/3 cup semisweet chips, 2/3 cup white chips and walnuts. Spread dough in prepared pan.

3. Bake 23 to 25 minutes or until center is firm. *Do not overbake.* Sprinkle with remaining 1/3 cup semisweet chips and 1/3 cup white chips. Let stand until chips soften; spread evenly over bars. Cool in pan on wire rack until chocolate is set. Cut into bars or triangles.

# double striped peanut butter oatmeal cookies

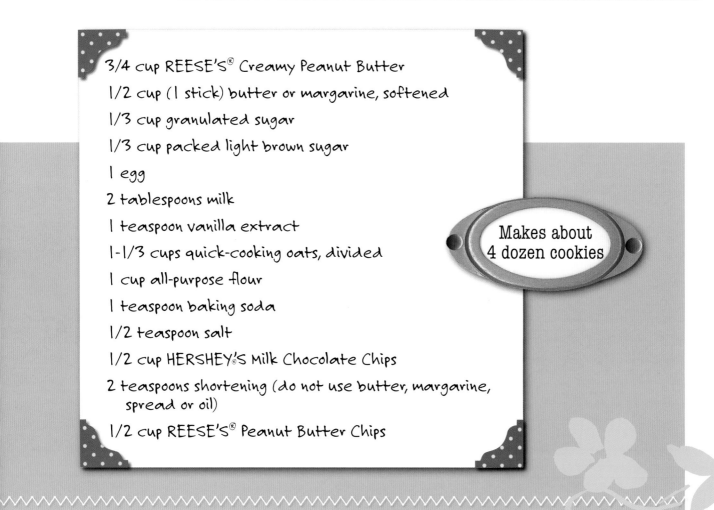

3/4 cup REESE'S® Creamy Peanut Butter

1/2 cup (1 stick) butter or margarine, softened

1/3 cup granulated sugar

1/3 cup packed light brown sugar

1 egg

2 tablespoons milk

1 teaspoon vanilla extract

1-1/3 cups quick-cooking oats, divided

1 cup all-purpose flour

1 teaspoon baking soda

1/2 teaspoon salt

1/2 cup HERSHEY'S® Milk Chocolate Chips

2 teaspoons shortening (do not use butter, margarine, spread or oil)

1/2 cup REESE'S® Peanut Butter Chips

Makes about
4 dozen cookies

*Spray tines of fork before pressing into cookies to prevent sticking. The crisscross pattern is a classic decoration for peanut butter cookies.*

1. Heat oven to 350°F. Beat peanut butter and butter in large bowl until well blended. Add granulated sugar and brown sugar; beat until fluffy. Add egg, milk and vanilla; beat well. Stir together 1/2 cup oats, flour, baking soda and salt; gradually beat into peanut butter mixture.

2. Shape dough into 1-inch balls. Roll in remaining oats; place on ungreased cookie sheet. Flatten cookies with tines of fork to form a crisscross pattern.

3. Bake 10 to 12 minutes or until lightly browned. Cool slightly; remove from cookie sheet to wire rack. Cool completely.

4. Place chocolate chips and 1 teaspoon shortening in medium microwave-safe container. Microwave at medium (50%) 30 seconds; stir. If necessary, microwave at medium an additional 10 seconds at a time, stirring after each heating, until chocolate is melted and smooth when stirred. Drizzle over cookies. Repeat procedure with peanut butter chips and remaining 1 teaspoon shortening. Allow drizzles to set.

# butterscotch toffee gingersnap squares

40 gingersnap cookies

1/3 cup butter, melted

1 can (14 ounces) sweetened condensed milk

1-1/2 teaspoons vanilla

1 cup butterscotch chips

1/2 cup pecan pieces

1/2 cup chopped peanuts

1/2 cup milk chocolate toffee bits

1/2 cup mini semisweet chocolate chips

**Makes 3 dozen bars**

1. Preheat oven to 350°F. Line 13×9-inch baking pan with foil, leaving 1-inch overhang. Spray foil with nonstick cooking spray.

2. Place cookies in food processor; process until crumbs form. Measure 2 cups.

3. Combine 2 cups crumbs and butter in medium bowl; mix well. Press crumb mixture evenly into bottom of prepared pan. Bake 4 to 5 minutes or until light brown around edges.

4. Combine condensed milk and vanilla in small bowl; pour over warm crust. Sprinkle with butterscotch chips, pecans, peanuts, toffee bits and chocolate chips. Press down gently.

5. Bake 15 to 18 minutes or until bubbly and golden. Cool completely in pan on wire rack. Remove from pan using foil; cut into bars. Store in airtight container.

# chocolate chunk cookies

2-3/4 cups flour

1 teaspoon baking soda

1/4 teaspoon salt

3/4 cup butter or margarine, softened

3/4 cup firmly packed brown sugar

1/2 cup KARO® Light or Dark Corn Syrup

1 egg

1 teaspoon vanilla

1 package (8 ounces) semi sweet chocolate, cut into
1/2-inch chunks, divided

1 cup chopped pecans, divided

Makes
36 cookies

In bowl combine flour, baking soda and salt.

In mixing bowl with mixer at medium speed beat butter and sugar until fluffy. Gradually beat in corn syrup. Beat in egg and vanilla. Gradually beat in flour mixture until just combined.

Stir in half of the chocolate chunks and pecans.

Drop dough by rounded tablespoonfuls onto ungreased baking sheets. Sprinkle with remaining chocolate chunks and pecans.

Bake in 350°F oven 8 to 10 minutes or until lightly browned. Cool on wire rack.

**Cook Time:** 10 minutes

*Classic* goodies

# Global flavors

## english toffee bars

2 cups all-purpose flour

1 cup packed light brown sugar

1/2 cup (1 stick) cold butter

1 cup pecan halves

Toffee Topping (recipe follows)

1 cup HERSHEY'S Milk Chocolate Chips

**Makes about 36 bars**

1. Heat oven to 350°F.

2. Combine flour and brown sugar in large bowl. With pastry blender or fork, cut in butter until fine crumbs form (a few large crumbs may remain). Press mixture into bottom of ungreased 13×9×2-inch baking pan. Sprinkle pecans over crust. Prepare Toffee Topping; drizzle evenly over pecans and crust.

3. Bake 20 to 22 minutes or until topping is bubbly and golden; remove from oven. Immediately sprinkle milk chocolate chips evenly over top; press gently onto surface. Cool completely in pan on wire rack. Cut into bars.

**Toffee Topping:** Combine 2/3 cup butter and 1/3 cup packed light brown sugar in small saucepan; cook over medium heat, stirring constantly, until mixture comes to a boil. Continue boiling, stirring constantly, 30 seconds. Use immediately.

1 cup sugar

4 eggs

1-1/2 cups all-purpose flour

1 cup (6 ounces) ground almonds*

1/3 cup candied lemon peel, finely chopped

1/3 cup candied orange peel, finely chopped

1-1/2 teaspoons ground cinnamon

1 teaspoon grated lemon peel

1/2 teaspoon ground cardamom

1/2 teaspoon ground nutmeg

1/4 teaspoon ground cloves

3 squares (1 ounce each) bittersweet or semisweet chocolate, coarsely chopped

1 tablespoon butter

*To grind almonds, place in food processor or blender. Process using on/off pulsing action until finely ground, but not pasty.*

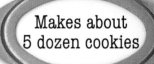

Makes about 5 dozen cookies

*Chocolate should be stored, tightly wrapped, in a cool dry place. Ideally dark chocolate can be stored for years, but milk and white chocolate shouldn't be kept for longer than 9 months.*

1. Beat sugar and eggs in large bowl with electric mixer at high speed 10 minutes.

2. Meanwhile, combine flour, almonds, candied lemon and orange peels, cinnamon, grated lemon peel, cardamom, nutmeg and cloves in another large bowl. Add egg mixture; stir until well blended. Cover; refrigerate 12 hours or overnight.

3. Preheat oven to 350°F. Line cookie sheets with parchment paper or grease and dust with flour. Drop dough by rounded teaspoonfuls 2 inches apart onto prepared cookie sheets. Bake 8 to 10 minutes or just until browned. *Do not overbake.* Remove to wire racks; cool slightly.

4. Meanwhile, combine chocolate and butter in small microwavable bowl. Microwave on HIGH 30 seconds; stir. Repeat as necessary until chocolate is melted and mixture is smooth. Spread over tops of warm cookies. Let stand until glaze is set. Store in airtight container.

# dulce de leche blondies

2 cups all-purpose flour

1 teaspoon baking soda

1 teaspoon salt

1 cup (2 sticks) butter, softened

1 cup firmly packed brown sugar

2 eggs

1-1/2 teaspoons vanilla

1 package (14 ounces) caramels

1/2 cup evaporated milk

**Makes about 3 dozen bars**

1. Preheat oven to 350°F. Grease 13×9-inch baking pan. Sift flour, baking soda and salt into medium bowl; set aside.

2. Beat butter and brown sugar in large bowl with electric mixer at medium speed until creamy. Add eggs and vanilla; beat until smooth. Gradually stir in flour mixture. Spread half of batter in prepared pan. Bake about 8 minutes; cool 5 minutes on wire rack.

3. Melt caramels with evaporated milk in nonstick saucepan over very low heat until caramels are melted and mixture is smooth. Reserve 2 tablespoons mixture; pour remaining caramel mixture over baked bottom layer. Drop tablespoonfuls of remaining batter over caramel layer; swirl slightly with knife.

4. Bake 25 minutes or until golden brown. Cool completely in pan on wire rack. Cut into bars. Reheat reserved caramel; drizzle over bars.

# chinese almond cookies

1 package (about 18 ounces) yellow cake mix

5 tablespoons butter, melted

1 egg

1-1/2 teaspoons almond extract

30 whole almonds

1 egg yolk

1 teaspoon water

1. Beat cake mix, butter, egg and almond extract in large bowl with electric mixer at medium speed until well blended. Shape dough into ball; wrap in plastic wrap and chill 4 hours or overnight.

2. Preheat oven to 350°F. Spray cookie sheets with nonstick cooking spray; set aside.

3. Shape dough into 1-inch balls; place 2 inches apart on prepared cookie sheets. Press 1 almond into center of each ball, flattening slightly.

4. Whisk together egg yolk and water in small bowl. Brush tops of cookies with egg yolk mixture. Bake 10 to 12 minutes or until lightly browned. Cool 5 minutes on cookie sheets. Remove to wire rack; cool completely.

**Prep Time:** 15 minutes

**Bake Time:** 10 minutes

**Chill Time:** 4 hours

Makes about
2-1/2 dozen
cookies

# chewy brown butter pine nut triangles

3/4 cup (1-1/2 sticks) butter

1-1/2 cups sugar

2 eggs

1/2 teaspoon vanilla

2 cups all-purpose flour

1/2 teaspoon baking powder

1/4 teaspoon salt

3/4 cup pine nuts

Powdered sugar (optional)

**Makes 3 dozen triangles**

1. Preheat oven 350°F. Line 13×9-inch baking pan with foil, leaving 1-inch overhang. Spray foil with nonstick cooking spray.

2. Melt butter in small heavy saucepan over medium heat. Bring to a boil, stirring constantly with wooden spoon. Continue boiling until butter begins to color and form small brown bits on bottom of saucepan. Remove pan from heat. Carefully pour hot butter into large mixing bowl. Let cool 30 minutes.

3. Add sugar to butter in bowl. Beat with electric mixer at medium speed 1 minute. Add eggs, one at a time. Stir in vanilla. Add flour, baking powder and salt; beat until just blended.

4. Spread cookie dough evenly into prepared pan. Sprinkle with nuts. Press down to adhere nuts to dough. Bake 25 to 28 minutes or until golden brown. Cool completely in pan on wire rack.

5. Remove from pan using foil; cut into squares. Cut each square in half diagonally to form triangles. Dust with powdered sugar, if desired. Store in airtight container.

Browned butter adds a wonderful nutty background flavor to baked goods. Melted butter may be substituted.

Makes about
5 dozen cookies

# danish cookie rings (vanillekranser)

1/2 cup blanched almonds

2 cups all-purpose flour

3/4 cup sugar

1/4 teaspoon baking powder

1 cup (2 sticks) cold butter, cut into small pieces

1 egg

1 tablespoon milk

1 tablespoon vanilla

15 candied red cherries

15 candied green cherries

1. Grease cookie sheets; set aside. Process almonds in food processor using on/off pulsing action until finely ground but not pasty. Place almonds, flour, sugar and baking powder in large bowl. Cut butter into flour mixture with pastry blender or 2 knives until mixture is crumbly.

2. Beat egg, milk and vanilla in small bowl until well blended. Add egg mixture to flour mixture; stir until soft dough forms.

3. Spoon dough into pastry bag fitted with medium star tip. Pipe 3-inch rings 2 inches apart on prepared cookie sheets. Refrigerate 15 minutes or until firm.

4. Preheat oven to 375°F. Cut red cherries into quarters. Cut green cherries into halves; cut each half into 4 slivers. Press red cherry quarter onto each ring where ends meet. Place green cherry sliver on either side of red cherry to form leaves. Bake 8 to 10 minutes or until golden. Remove to wire racks; cool completely. Store tightly covered at room temperature or freeze up to 3 months.

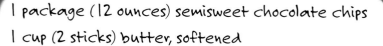

# aztec brownies

1 package (12 ounces) semisweet chocolate chips
1 cup (2 sticks) butter, softened
1 cup sugar
3 eggs
1 tablespoon instant coffee granules or powder
1 tablespoon vanilla
3/4 cup all-purpose flour
2 teaspoons baking powder
1 teaspoon ground cinnamon
1 to 2 teaspoons chili powder
1/2 teaspoon salt
3/4 cup sliced almonds

Makes
3 dozen
brownies

*For easier cutting, refrigerate the brownies a few hours before cutting.*

1. Preheat oven to 350°F. Line 13×9-inch baking pan with foil; spray foil with nonstick cooking spray.

2. Place chocolate chips and butter in medium microwavable bowl; microwave on HIGH 30 seconds. Stir until mixture is smooth. Microwave at 10-second intervals, if necessary, until mixture is melted and smooth.

3. Whisk sugar, eggs, coffee granules and vanilla in medium bowl until well blended. Stir in warm chocolate mixture; set aside to cool 10 minutes. Whisk flour, baking powder, cinnamon, chili powder and salt in large bowl; stir into chocolate mixture until well blended. Pour batter into prepared pan.

4. Bake 15 minutes; sprinkle with almonds. Bake 20 minutes longer or until toothpick inserted into center comes out almost clean. *Do not overbake.* Cool completely in pan on wire rack. Cut into squares or triangles.

**Prep Time:** 20 minutes
**Bake Time:** 35 minutes

# irish soda bread cookies

2 cups all-purpose flour

1/2 teaspoon baking soda

1/4 teaspoon salt

1/2 cup (1 stick) butter, softened

1/2 cup sugar

1 egg

3/4 cup currants

1 teaspoon caraway seeds

1/3 cup buttermilk

1. Preheat oven to 350°F. Line 2 cookie sheets with parchment paper.

2. Combine flour, baking soda and salt in medium bowl.

3. Beat butter and sugar in large bowl with electric mixer at medium speed until fluffy. Add egg; beat 1 minute until combined. Add flour mixture; beat on low speed until combined. Add currants and caraway seeds; mix well. Add buttermilk; mix until combined.

4. Drop dough by tablespoonfuls 1 inch apart onto prepared cookie sheets. Bake 12 to 15 minutes or until light brown. Remove to wire racks; serve warm.

Makes about
3 dozen cookies

# molded scottish shortbread

1-1/2 cups all-purpose flour

1/4 teaspoon salt

3/4 cup (1-1/2 sticks) butter, softened

1/3 cup sugar

1 egg

Makes 8 to 10 servings

Butter can be stored in the refrigerator up to 1 month. Be sure to wrap it airtight, as butter readily absorbs flavors and odors from other items in the refrigerator.

1. Preheat oven to temperature recommended by shortbread mold manufacturer. Spray 10-inch ceramic shortbread mold with nonstick cooking spray.

2. Combine flour and salt in medium bowl. Beat butter and sugar in large bowl with electric mixer at medium speed until light and fluffy. Add egg; beat until well blended. Gradually add flour mixture, beating at low speed until well blended.

3. Press dough firmly into mold. Bake, cool and remove from mold according to manufacturer's directions.

**Scottish Shortbread Cookies:** If shortbread mold is not available, preheat oven to 350°F. Shape dough into 1-inch balls. Place 2 inches apart on ungreased cookie sheets; press with fork to flatten. Bake 18 to 20 minutes or until edges are lightly browned. Cool 2 minutes on cookie sheets. Remove to wire racks; cool completely. Makes 2 dozen cookies.

# finnish nut logs (pahkinaleivat)

1 cup (2 sticks) butter, softened

1/2 cup plus 1/3 cup sugar, divided

3 eggs

1/2 teaspoon ground cardamom

1/2 teaspoon almond extract

2-1/4 to 2-1/2 cups all-purpose flour

1 cup finely chopped almonds

Makes about
4 dozen cookies

1. Beat butter and 1/2 cup sugar in large bowl with electric mixer at medium speed until light and fluffy. Beat in 1 egg, cardamom and almond extract until well blended. Gradually add 1-1/2 cups flour, beating at low speed until well blended. Stir in enough remaining flour with spoon to form soft dough. Shape dough into disc; wrap tightly in plastic wrap. Refrigerate until firm, at least 30 minutes or overnight.

2. Grease cookie sheets. Divide dough into 8 equal pieces. With floured hands, shape each piece into 12×1/2-inch rope. Cut each rope into six 2-inch logs; place on prepared cookie sheets. Refrigerate 30 minutes.

3. Preheat oven to 350°F. Combine almonds and remaining 1/3 cup sugar in medium bowl. Beat remaining 2 eggs with fork in shallow dish until foamy; dip logs into beaten egg mixture. Roll in nut mixture to coat; return to cookie sheets.

4. Bake 15 minutes or until lightly browned. Remove to wire racks; cool completely. Store tightly covered at room temperature or freeze up to 3 months.

# chocolate hazelnut wedges

1-1/2 cups hazelnuts

1-1/2 cups (3 sticks) butter, softened

1 cup powdered sugar

1 teaspoon vanilla

3 cups all-purpose flour

1/2 teaspoon salt

1-1/4 cups mini semisweet chocolate chips, divided

1/3 cup chocolate hazelnut spread

*Dough can be prepared up to 2 days before baking; wrap pie pans with plastic wrap and store in refrigerator. Bake as directed below.*

1. Preheat oven to 350°F. Place hazelnuts on baking sheet; bake 12 minutes. Place warm nuts on clean dish towel and rub nuts inside towel to remove most of papery skins. Cool; finely chop nuts. Measure 1 cup nuts; reserve remaining nuts for topping. *Reduce oven temperature to 325°F.*

2. Beat butter, powdered sugar and vanilla in large bowl with electric mixer at medium speed until light and fluffy. Sift flour and salt over butter mixture; beat until blended. Add 3/4 cup chocolate chips and 1 cup chopped nuts; stir until well blended. Divide dough in half; pat each half evenly into ungreased 9-inch pie pan. Score dough into 12 wedges per pan.

3. Bake 25 minutes or until edges are lightly browned. Cool completely in pans on wire racks. Cut cooled cookies into wedges along score lines.

4. Place remaining 1/2 cup chocolate chips and chocolate hazelnut spread in small resealable food storage bag. Microwave on HIGH 20 seconds; knead bag until smooth. Cut 1/4 inch from one corner of bag and drizzle mixture over cookies. Sprinkle with reserved nuts.

Makes 2 dozen cookies

# coconut almond biscotti

2-1/2 cups all-purpose flour

1-1/3 cups unsweetened shredded coconut

3/4 cup sliced almonds

2/3 cup sugar

2 teaspoons baking powder

1/2 teaspoon salt

1/2 cup (1 stick) butter, melted

1 egg, at room temperature

1 egg white, at room temperature

1 teaspoon vanilla

Makes 2 dozen biscotti

*Biscotti makes a fantastic afternoon snack to dip into a steamy cappuccino or cup of hot tea.*

1. Place rack in center of oven. Preheat oven to 350°F. Line cookie sheet with parchment paper.

2. Combine flour, coconut, almonds, sugar, baking powder and salt in large bowl; mix well.

3. Beat butter, egg, egg white and vanilla in large bowl with electric mixer at medium speed until well blended. Add flour mixture; beat at low speed until combined.

4. Divide dough into 2 equal pieces. Shape each piece of dough into 8×3-inch loaf with lightly floured hands. Place loaves 2 inches apart on cookie sheet.

5. Bake 26 to 28 minutes or until golden brown and set. Cool 10 minutes on cookie sheet on wire rack. Slice each loaf into 1/2-inch-thick slices with serrated knife. Place slices, cut side up, on cookie sheets. Bake 20 minutes or until firm and golden. Remove to wire rack; cool completely.

# norwegian almond squares

**Makes about 3-1/2 dozen squares**

1-3/4 cups all-purpose flour

1 cup sugar

1 cup (2 sticks) butter, softened

1/4 cup ground almonds

1 egg

1 teaspoon ground cinnamon

1/2 teaspoon salt

1 egg white

3/4 cup sliced almonds

1. Preheat oven to 350°F. Beat flour, sugar, butter, ground almonds, egg, cinnamon and salt in medium bowl. Beat with electric mixer at low speed 2 to 3 minutes or until well mixed. Press dough onto ungreased cookie sheet to 1/16-inch thickness.

2. Beat egg white with fork in small bowl until foamy. Brush over dough; sprinkle with sliced almonds. Bake 12 to 15 minutes or until very lightly browned. Immediately cut into 2-inch squares. Remove to wire rack; cool completely. Store in tightly covered container.

# parmesan and pine nut shortbread

1/2 cup all-purpose flour

1/3 cup whole-wheat flour

1/3 cup cornmeal

1/4 teaspoon salt

1/2 cup (1 stick) butter, softened

1/2 cup shredded Parmesan cheese

1/3 cup sugar

1/4 cup pine nuts

**Makes about 2-1/2 dozen cookies**

1. Line cookie sheets with parchment paper; set aside. Combine flours, cornmeal and salt in small bowl.

2. Beat butter, cheese and sugar in medium bowl with electric mixer at high speed until light and fluffy. Scrape down bowl. Gradually add flour mixture at low speed, beating well after each addition. Shape dough into 8×2-inch log. Wrap in plastic wrap and chill 30 minutes.

3. Preheat oven to 375°F. Cut dough into 1/3-inch slices with sharp knife. Arrange 1 inch apart on prepared cookie sheets. Press 3 to 5 pine nuts on each slice. Bake 11 to 13 minutes or until firm and lightly browned. Cool 5 minutes on cookie sheets. Remove to wire rack; cool completely.

# irish flag bar cookies

1-1/2 cups all-purpose flour

1 teaspoon baking powder

1/2 teaspoon salt

3/4 cup granulated sugar

3/4 cup packed light brown sugar

1/2 cup (1 stick) butter, softened

2 eggs

2 teaspoons vanilla

1 package (12 ounces) semisweet chocolate chips

Prepared white frosting

Green and orange food coloring and decorating gels

Makes 2 dozen cookies

1. Preheat oven to 350°F. Grease 13×9-inch baking pan. Combine flour, baking powder and salt in small bowl.

2. Beat granulated sugar, brown sugar and butter in large bowl with electric mixer at medium speed until light and fluffy. Beat in eggs and vanilla. Add flour mixture; beat at low speed until well blended. Stir in chocolate chips. Spread batter evenly in prepared pan. Bake 25 to 30 minutes or until golden brown. Cool completely in pan on wire rack. Cut into bars.

3. Divide frosting among 3 small bowls. Tint 1 with green food coloring and 1 with orange food coloring. Leave remaining frosting white. Frost individual cookies as shown in photo.

# Chocolate obsession

## cocoa raisin-chip cookies

1-1/2 cups all-purpose flour

1/4 cup unsweetened cocoa powder

1 teaspoon baking powder

1/2 teaspoon salt

1 cup packed light brown sugar

1/2 cup granulated sugar

1/2 cup (1 stick) butter, softened

1/2 cup shortening

2 eggs

1 teaspoon vanilla

1-1/2 cups semisweet chocolate chips

1 cup raisins

3/4 cup chopped walnuts

Makes 4 dozen cookies

1. Preheat oven to 350°F. Line cookies sheets with parchment paper or lightly grease and dust with flour.

2. Combine flour, cocoa, baking powder and salt in medium bowl. Beat brown sugar, granulated sugar, butter and shortening in large bowl with electric mixer at medium speed until light and creamy. Add eggs, one at a time, beating well after each addition. Beat in vanilla. Add flour mixture; beat until well blended. Stir in chocolate chips, raisins and walnuts. Drop dough by tablespoonfuls onto prepared cookie sheets.

3. Bake 10 to 12 minutes or until set. Remove to wire racks; cool completely.

# o'henrietta bars

MAZOLA PURE® Cooking Spray

1/2 cup (1 stick) butter or margarine, softened

1/2 cup packed brown sugar

1/2 cup KARO® Light or Dark Corn Syrup

1 teaspoon vanilla

3 cups quick oats, uncooked

1/2 cup (3 ounces) semi-sweet chocolate chips

1/4 cup creamy peanut butter

1. Preheat oven to 350°F. Spray 8- or 9-inch square baking pan with cooking spray.

2. Beat butter, brown sugar, corn syrup and vanilla in large bowl with mixer at medium speed until smooth. Stir in oats. Press into prepared pan.

3. Bake 25 minutes or until center is barely firm. Cool on wire rack 5 minutes.

4. Sprinkle with chocolate chips; top with small spoonfuls of peanut butter. Let stand 5 minutes; spread peanut butter and chocolate over bars, swirling to marble.

5. Cool completely on wire rack before cutting. Cut into bars; refrigerate 15 minutes to set topping.

**Prep Time:** 20 minutes

**Bake Time:** 25 minutes, plus cooling

Makes
24 bars

# rich cocoa crinkle cookies

2 cups granulated sugar

3/4 cup vegetable oil

1 cup HERSHEY'S Cocoa

4 eggs

2 teaspoons vanilla extract

2-1/3 cups all-purpose flour

2 teaspoons baking powder

1/2 teaspoon salt

Powdered sugar

**Makes about 6 dozen cookies**

1. Combine granulated sugar and oil in large bowl; add cocoa, beating until well blended. Beat in eggs and vanilla. Stir together flour, baking powder and salt. Gradually add to cocoa mixture, beating well.

2. Cover; refrigerate until dough is firm enough to handle, at least 6 hours.

3. Heat oven to 350°F. Grease cookie sheet or line with parchment paper. Shape dough into 1-inch balls; roll in powdered sugar to coat. Place about 2 inches apart on prepared cookie sheet.

4. Bake 10 to 12 minutes or until almost no indentation remains when touched lightly and tops are crackled. Cool slightly. Remove from cookie sheet to wire rack. Cool completely.

# almond shortbread cookies with chocolate filling

3/4 cup sliced almonds, toasted*

1 cup (2 sticks) butter or margarine, softened

3/4 cup sugar

3 egg yolks

3/4 teaspoon almond extract

2 cups all-purpose flour

Chocolate Filling (recipe follows)

Powdered sugar (optional)

*To toast almonds: Heat oven to 350°F. Spread almonds in thin layer in shallow baking pan. Bake 8 to 10 minutes, stirring occasionally, until light golden brown; cool.

Cookie dough won't stick to cookie cutters if you spritz them first with nonstick cooking spray. Or, try dipping cutters in flour or powdered sugar whenever dough begins to stick.

Makes about 44 sandwich cookies

1. Finely chop almonds; set aside.

2. Beat butter and sugar in large bowl until creamy. Add egg yolks and almond extract; beat well. Gradually add flour, beating until well blended. Stir in almonds. Refrigerate dough 1 to 2 hours or until firm enough to handle.

3. Heat oven to 350°F. On well-floured surface, roll about one-fourth of dough to about 1/8-inch thickness (keep remaining dough in refrigerator). Using 2-inch round cookie cutter, cut into equal number of rounds. Place on ungreased cookie sheet.

4. Bake 8 to 10 minutes or until almost set. Cool slightly; remove from cookie sheet to wire rack. Cool completely. Spread about one measuring teaspoonful Chocolate Filling onto bottom of one cookie. Top with second cookie; gently press together. Repeat with remaining cookies. Allow to set, about 1 hour. Lightly sift powdered sugar over top of cookies, if desired. Cover; store at room temperature.

**Chocolate Filling:** Combine 1 cup HERSHEY'S Milk Chocolate Chips** and 1/3 cup whipping cream in small saucepan. Stir constantly over low heat until mixture is smooth. Remove from heat. Cool about 20 minutes or until slightly thickened and spreadable. Makes about 1 cup filling.

*\*\*HERSHEY'S SPECIAL DARK® Chocolate Chips or HERSHEY'S Semi-Sweet Chocolate Chips may also be used.*

# double chocolate coconut oatmeal cookies

1 cup shortening

1-3/4 cups packed light brown sugar

3 eggs

2 teaspoons vanilla extract

1-1/3 cups all-purpose flour

1/2 cup HERSHEY'S Cocoa

2 teaspoons baking soda

1/4 teaspoon salt

1/2 cup water

3 cups rolled oats or quick-cooking oats

2 cups (12-ounce package) HERSHEY'S SPECIAL DARK Chocolate Chips or HERSHEY'S Semi-Sweet Chocolate Chips, divided

2 cups MOUNDS® Sweetened Coconut Flakes, divided

1 cup coarsely chopped nuts

**Makes about 2-1/2 dozen cookies**

1. Beat shortening, brown sugar, eggs and vanilla in large bowl until well blended. Stir together flour, cocoa, baking soda and salt; add alternately with water to shortening mixture. Stir in oats, 1 cup chocolate chips, 1 cup coconut and nuts, blending well. Cover; refrigerate 2 hours.

2. Heat oven to 350°F. Lightly grease cookie sheet or line with parchment paper. Using 1/4-cup ice cream scoop or measuring cup, drop dough about 4 inches apart onto prepared cookie sheet. Sprinkle cookie tops with remaining coconut. Top with remaining chocolate chips (about 9 chips per cookie); lightly press into dough.

3. Bake 10 to 12 minutes or until set (do not overbake). Cool slightly; remove from cookie sheet to wire rack. Cool completely.

# chewy peanut butter brownies

3/4 cup (1-1/2 sticks) butter, melted

3/4 cup creamy peanut butter

1-3/4 cups sugar

2 teaspoons vanilla

4 eggs, lightly beaten

1-1/4 cups all-purpose flour

1/2 teaspoon baking powder

1/4 teaspoon salt

1/4 cup unsweetened cocoa powder

**Makes about 3 dozen brownies**

1. Preheat oven to 350°F. Grease 13×9-inch baking pan.

2. Beat butter and peanut butter in large bowl with electric mixer at low speed 3 minutes or until well blended. Add sugar and vanilla; beat until blended. Add eggs; beat until well blended. Stir in flour, baking powder and salt just until blended. Reserve 1-3/4 cups batter. Stir cocoa into remaining batter.

3. Spread chocolate batter in prepared pan. Top with reserved batter. Bake 30 minutes or until edges begin to pull away from sides of pan. Cool completely in pan on wire rack. Cut into bars.

# chocolate 'n' oat bars

1 cup all-purpose flour

1 cup quick-cooking oats

3/4 cup firmly packed light brown sugar

1/2 cup (1 stick) butter or margarine, softened

1 (14-ounce) can EAGLE BRAND® Sweetened Condensed Milk (NOT evaporated milk)

1 cup chopped nuts

1 cup (6 ounces) semisweet chocolate chips

1. Preheat oven to 350°F (325°F for glass dish). In large bowl, combine flour, oats, brown sugar and butter; mix well. (Mixture will be crumbly.) Reserve 1/2 cup oat mixture and press remainder on bottom of 13×9-inch baking pan. Bake 10 minutes.

2. Pour EAGLE BRAND® evenly over crust. Sprinkle with nuts and chocolate chips. Top with reserved oat mixture; press down firmly.

3. Bake 25 minutes or until lightly browned. Cool. Chill if desired. Cut into bars. Store leftovers covered at room temperature.

**Prep Time:** 15 minutes

**Bake Time:** 35 minutes

Makes
2 to 3 dozen
bars

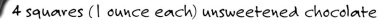

# chunky double chocolate cookies

4 squares (1 ounce each) unsweetened chocolate

1 cup all-purpose flour

1 cup whole wheat flour

1-1/2 teaspoons baking powder

1/2 teaspoon salt

1-1/2 cups packed brown sugar

3/4 cup (1-1/2 sticks) butter, softened

1 teaspoon vanilla

2 eggs

12 ounces white chocolate, chopped or 1 package (12 ounces) white chocolate chips

1 cup chopped nuts (optional)

Makes about 3-1/2 dozen cookies

1. Preheat oven to 350°F. Melt unsweetened chocolate according to package directions; cool slightly.

2. Combine all-purpose flour, whole wheat flour, baking powder and salt in medium bowl. Beat brown sugar, butter and vanilla in large bowl with electric mixer at medium speed until light and fluffy. Add eggs; beat until well blended. Beat in melted chocolate. Gradually add flour mixture, mixing well after each addition. Stir in white chocolate and nuts, if desired. Drop dough by heaping tablespoonfuls 2 inches apart onto ungreased cookie sheets.

3. Bake 11 to 12 minutes or just until set. Cool 1 minute on cookie sheets. Remove to wire racks; cool completely. Store in tightly covered container up to 1 week.

Chocolate obsession

# peanut butter crème blossoms

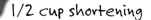

1/2 cup shortening

3/4 cup REESE'S® Creamy Peanut Butter

1/3 cup granulated sugar

1/3 cup packed light brown sugar

1 egg

2 tablespoons milk

1 teaspoon vanilla extract

1-1/2 cups all-purpose flour

1 teaspoon baking soda

1/2 teaspoon salt

1 can (16 ounces) vanilla or chocolate frosting

1-1/3 cups (8-ounce package) REESE'S® Milk Chocolate Baking Pieces Filled with Peanut Butter Crème

**Makes about 4-1/2 dozen cookies**

1. Heat oven to 375°F.

2. Beat shortening and peanut butter in large bowl until blended. Add granulated sugar and brown sugar; beat until fluffy. Add egg, milk and vanilla. Beat well. Combine flour, baking soda and salt; gradually add to peanut butter mixture. Beat well. Shape dough into 1-inch balls; place on ungreased cookie sheets.

3. Bake 8 to 10 minutes or until lightly browned. Immediately press bottom of large wooden spoon (about 1/2 inch in diameter) into center of each cookie, cookie will crack around edges. Remove from cookie sheet to wire rack; cool completely.

4. Spoon frosting into heavy-duty resealable plastic food storage bag. Cut off corner of bag about 1/4 inch from point; pipe frosting into indentations. Gently press 3 to 4 baking pieces in each filled cookie.

# oatmeal s'mores cookies

2/3 cup mini marshmallows

Basic Oatmeal Dough (page 148)

1 cup semisweet chocolate chips

3/4 cup coarse chocolate graham cracker crumbs

1. Cut marshmallows in half. Spread on baking sheet; freeze 1 hour.

2. Preheat oven to 350°F. Line cookie sheets with parchment paper.

3. Prepare Basic Oatmeal Cookie Dough. Stir in chocolate chips and marshmallows.

4. Drop dough by rounded tablespoonfuls onto prepared cookie sheets. Sprinkle with graham cracker crumbs; press lightly. Bake 14 to 16 minutes or until puffed and golden. Cool 5 minutes on cookie sheets. Remove to wire racks; cool completely.

**Variation:** To make sandwich cookies, spread 1 tablespoon marshmallow crème onto flat side of one cookie. Spread 1 tablespoon prepared chocolate fudge frosting on flat side of second cookie. Press cookies together lightly; repeat with remaining cookies, marshmallow crème and frosting. Makes about 20 sandwiches.

Makes about
3 dozen cookies

# black forest bars

1 package (about 18 ounces) dark chocolate cake mix

1/2 cup (1 stick) unsalted butter, melted

1 egg

1/2 teaspoon almond extract

1-1/4 cups sliced almonds, divided

1 jar (about 16 ounces) maraschino cherries, well drained

1/2 cup semisweet chocolate chips

1. Preheat oven to 350°F. Line 13×9-inch baking pan with foil; set aside.

2. Beat cake mix, butter, egg and extract in large bowl with electric mixer at medium speed until blended. Stir in 3/4 cup almonds.

3. Press dough into bottom of prepared pan. Top evenly with cherries. Bake 20 to 25 minutes or until toothpick inserted into center comes out clean. Cool completely in pan on wire rack.

4. Place chocolate chips in small resealable food storage bag; seal bag. Microwave on HIGH 1 to 1-1/2 minutes, kneading bag every 30 seconds until melted and smooth. Cut tiny corner from bag; drizzle chocolate over brownies. Sprinkle with reserved almonds. Cut into bars to serve.

**Prep Time:** 10 minutes

**Bake Time:** 20 to 25 minutes

Makes about 2 dozen bars

# chocolate oat shortbread

1 cup (2 sticks) butter, softened

1 cup powdered sugar

2 teaspoons vanilla extract

1-1/2 cups all-purpose flour

1 cup quick-cooking or old-fashioned oats, uncooked

1/4 cup unsweetened cocoa powder

1 teaspoon ground cinnamon

1-3/4 cups "M&M's"® Chocolate Mini Baking Bits, divided

**Makes 36 to 48 bars**

Preheat oven to 325°F. Lightly grease 13×9×2-inch pan. Cream butter and sugar until light and fluffy; add vanilla. Combine flour, oats, cocoa powder and cinnamon; blend into creamed mixture. Stir in 1 cup "M&M's"® Chocolate Mini Baking Bits; press dough into prepared pan. Sprinkle remaining 3/4 cup "M&M's"® Chocolate Mini Baking Bits over dough; press in lightly. Bake 20 to 25 minutes or until set. Cool completely; cut into triangles.

# extra-chocolatey brownie cookies

2 cups all-purpose flour

1/2 cup unsweetened Dutch-process cocoa powder

1 teaspoon baking soda

3/4 teaspoon salt

1 cup (2 sticks) butter, softened

1 cup firmly packed brown sugar

1/2 cup granulated sugar

2 eggs

2 teaspoon vanilla

1 package (11-1/2 ounces) semisweet chocolate chunks or chips

2 cups coarsely chopped walnuts or pecans

Makes 3 dozen cookies

1. Preheat oven to 375°F. Whisk flour, cocoa, baking soda and salt in medium bowl until well blended.

2. Beat butter in large bowl with electric mixer at medium speed about 1 minute or until light and fluffly. Add brown sugar and granulated sugar; beat 2 minutes or until fluffy. Add eggs and vanilla; beat until well blended. Add flour mixture; beat at low speed until blended. Stir in chocolate chunks and walnuts.

3. Drop dough by heaping tablespoonfuls about 2 inches apart onto ungreased cookie sheets. Flatten dough lightly with back of spoon.

4. Bake about 12 minutes or until edges are set. Cool cookies 2 minutes on cookie sheets. Remove to wire racks; cool completely. Store in airtight container at room temperature up to 4 days.

*Chocolate* **obsession**

In Dutch-process cocoa, the beans have been treated with an alkaline solution. This helps to neutralize cocoa's natural acidity, creating a more mellow flavored cocoa powder.

# original nestlé® toll house® chocolate chip cookies

2-1/4 cups all-purpose flour

1 teaspoon baking soda

1 teaspoon salt

1 cup (2 sticks) butter, softened

3/4 cup granulated sugar

3/4 cup packed brown sugar

1 teaspoon vanilla extract

2 eggs

2 cups (12-ounce package) NESTLÉ® TOLL HOUSE® Semi-Sweet Chocolate Morsels

1 cup chopped nuts

**PREHEAT** oven to 375°F.

**COMBINE** flour, baking soda and salt in small bowl. Beat butter, granulated sugar, brown sugar and vanilla extract in large mixer bowl until creamy. Add eggs, one at a time, beating well after each addition. Gradually beat in flour mixture. Stir in morsels and nuts. Drop by rounded tablespoonfuls onto ungreased baking sheets.

**BAKE** for 9 to 11 minutes or until golden brown. Cool on baking sheets for 2 minutes; remove to wire racks to cool completely.

Pan Cookie Variation: **GREASE** 15×10-inch jelly-roll pan. Prepare dough as above. Spread in prepared pan. Bake for 20 to 25 minutes or until golden brown. Cool in pan on wire rack. Makes 4 dozen bars.

1 package (about 18 ounces) white cake mix

1 cup toasted coconut,* plus additional for garnish

1/2 cup (1 stick) butter, melted

1 can (14 ounces) sweetened condensed milk

1 package (8 ounces) cream cheese, softened

Grated peel and juice of 3 limes

3 eggs

*To toast coconut, preheat oven to 350°F. Spread coconut on baking sheet. Bake 8 minutes or until golden. Remove to plate.

1. Preheat oven to 350°F. Line 13×9-inch pan with foil, leaving 1-inch overhang on sides.

2. Combine cake mix, 1 cup coconut and butter in large bowl until crumbly. Press mixture onto bottom of prepared pan. Bake 12 minutes or until light golden brown.

3. Beat sweetened condensed milk, cream cheese, lime peel and juice in another large bowl with electric mixer at medium speed 2 minutes or until well blended. Beat in eggs, one at a time. Spread mixture evenly over crust.

4. Bake 20 minutes or until filling is set and edges are lightly browned. Sprinkle with additional toasted coconut. Cool completely in pan on wire rack. Remove from pan using foil.

**Prep Time:** 10 minutes

**Bake Time:** 40 to 45 minutes

Makes about 2 dozen bars

# raspberry almond tarts

1 recipe Basic Short Dough (page 150)

1/2 teaspoon almond extract

1 can or tube (8 ounces) almond paste (do not use marzipan)

1/4 cup sugar

2 eggs

1/4 cup raspberry jam

Sliced almonds (optional)

1. Prepare Basic Short Dough, replacing vanilla with almond extract. Divide dough into 2 discs. Wrap discs in plastic wrap. Refrigerate at least 1 hour or until firm.

2. Preheat oven to 350°F. Remove dough from refrigerator; let stand 5 minutes. Lightly spray 48 mini (1-3/4-inch) muffin cups with nonstick cooking spray.

3. On lightly floured surface, roll half of dough to 1/8-inch thickness. Cut out circles with 2-1/2-inch round or fluted cookie cutter. Place circles into muffin cups. Press together any cracks. Repeat with remaining dough. Re-roll dough scraps once.

4. Beat almond paste and sugar until well blended in medium bowl with electric mixer at medium speed. Add eggs, one at a time; mix well. Fill tart shells with 1 teaspoon filling. Bake 18 to 20 minutes or until lightly browned. Cool completely in pans on wire rack.

5. To serve, spoon 1/2 teaspoon raspberry jam into each tart. Garnish with sliced almond. Store covered in refrigerator.

Makes
4 dozen tarts

# double chocolate cherry cookies

1-1/4 cups (2-1/2 sticks) butter or margarine, softened

1-3/4 cups sugar

2 eggs

1 tablespoon vanilla extract

3-1/2 cups all-purpose flour

3/4 cup unsweetened cocoa powder

1/2 teaspoon baking powder

1/2 teaspoon baking soda

1/4 teaspoon salt

2 (6-ounce) jars maraschino cherries (without stems), well drained and halved (about 72 cherry halves)

1 cup (6 ounces) semisweet chocolate chips

1 (14-ounce) can EAGLE BRAND® Sweetened Condensed Milk (NOT evaporated milk)

Makes about 6 dozen cookies

Forming cookie dough the same size and shape will promote even baking and browning. Using a small ice cream scoop or spoon may help to create even sized dough balls.

1. Preheat oven to 350°F. In large bowl, beat butter and sugar until fluffy; add eggs and vanilla; mix well.

2. In large bowl, combine flour, cocoa, baking powder, baking soda and salt; stir into butter mixture (dough will be stiff). Shape into 1-inch balls. Place 1 inch apart on ungreased baking sheets. Press cherry half into center of each cookie. Bake 8 to 10 minutes. Cool.

3. In heavy saucepan, over low heat, melt chocolate chips with EAGLE BRAND®; continue cooking about 3 minutes or until mixture thickens.

4. Frost each cookie, covering cherry. Store leftovers loosely covered at room temperature.

**Double Chocolate Pecan Cookies:** Prepare cookies as directed, omitting cherries; flatten. Bake as directed and frost tops. Garnish each cookie with pecan half.

**Prep:** 15 minutes

# apricot shortbread diamonds

1 package (about 18 ounces) yellow cake mix

2 eggs

1/4 cup vegetable oil

1 tablespoon water

1 cup apricot jam or orange marmalade

1 cup (about 6 ounces) diced dried apricots

1 cup sliced almonds

1. Preheat oven to 350°F. Line 15×10-inch jelly-roll pan with foil; spray lightly with cooking spray.

2. Beat cake mix, eggs, oil and water in large bowl with electric mixer at medium speed until well blended. Press dough into prepared pan with damp hands.

3. Place marmalade in small microwavable bowl. Heat on HIGH 20 seconds to soften. Spread marmalade evenly over dough; sprinkle with apricots and almonds.

4. Bake 25 minutes or until edges are browned and marmalade bubbles at edges. Cool completely in pan on wire rack. To cut cookies into diamonds, cut crosswise at 2-inch intervals, then cut diagonally at 2-inch intervals.

**Prep Time:** 20 minutes
**Bake Time:** 25 minutes

Makes
4 dozen bars

# piña colada cookie bars

1/2 cup (1 stick) butter, melted

1-1/2 cups graham cracker crumbs

1 can (14 ounces) sweetened condensed milk

2 tablespoons dark rum

2 cups white chocolate chips

1 cup shredded coconut

1/2 cup chopped macadamia nuts

1/2 cup chopped dried pineapple

**Makes 3 dozen bars**

1. Preheat oven to 350°F.

2. Pour butter into 13×9-inch baking pan, tilting pan to coat bottom. Sprinkle graham cracker crumbs evenly over butter. Blend sweetened condensed milk and rum in small bowl; pour over crumbs. Top with white chips, coconut, nuts and pineapple.

3. Bake 25 to 30 minutes or until edges are lightly browned. Cool in pan on wire rack. Cut into bars with serrated knife. Store loosely covered at room temperature.

# pear hazelnut bars

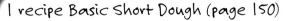

1 recipe Basic Short Dough (page 150)

1 tablespoon plus 1 teaspoon grated lemon peel, divided

4 cups chopped peeled fresh pears

1/2 cup raisins

2 tablespoons fresh lemon juice

1/2 cup plus 2 tablespoons all-purpose flour, divided

2 tablespoons granulated sugar

1-1/2 teaspoon ground cinnamon, divided

1/2 cup packed brown sugar

1/2 cup (1 stick) cold butter, cubed

1/2 cup uncooked old-fashioned oats

1/2 cup chopped hazelnuts

*The skin of a pear darkens and toughens when heated, so it should always be removed for baking. Use a vegetable peeler or sharp paring knife to remove the skin.*

Makes
3 dozen bars

1. Preheat oven to 350°F. Line 13×9-inch baking pan with foil, leaving 1-inch overhang. Spray foil with nonstick cooking spray.

2. Prepare Basic Short Dough, adding 1 tablespoon lemon peel to butter and sugar mixture. Press dough evenly into pan. Bake 25 minutes or until lightly browned. Set aside on wire rack.

3. Meanwhile, mix pears, raisins, lemon juice, 2 tablespoons flour, granulated sugar, 1/2 teaspoon cinnamon and remaining 1 teaspoon lemon peel in large bowl. Spread over warm crust.

4. Combine 1/2 cup flour, brown sugar and remaining 1/2 teaspoon cinnamon in medium bowl. Cut in butter with pastry blender or 2 knives until mixture resembles coarse crumbs. Stir in oats and hazelnuts. Sprinkle evenly over filling, lightly pressing into place.

5. Bake 30 to 32 minutes or until topping is golden brown. Cool completely in pan on wire rack.

6. Refrigerate bars at least 2 hours before serving. Remove from pan using foil; cut into 18 squares. Cut each square diagonally into triangles. Store covered in refrigerator.

# cobbled fruit bars

1-1/2 cups apple juice

1 cup (6 ounces) chopped dried apricots

1 cup (6 ounces) raisins

1 package (6 ounces) dried cherries

1 teaspoon cornstarch

1 teaspoon ground cinnamon

1 package (about 18 ounces) yellow cake mix

2 cups old-fashioned oats

3/4 cup (1-1/2 sticks) butter, melted

1 egg

Makes about 4 dozen bars

1. Combine apple juice, apricots, raisins, cherries, cornstarch and cinnamon in medium saucepan, stirring until cornstarch is dissolved. Bring to a boil over medium heat. Boil 5 minutes, stirring constantly. Remove from heat; cool to room temperature.

2. Preheat oven to 350°F. Line 15×10-inch jelly-roll pan with foil; spray lightly with cooking spray.

3. Combine cake mix and oats in large bowl; stir in butter. (Mixture may be dry and clumpy.) Add egg; stir until well blended.

4. Press three fourths of dough into prepared pan. Spread fruit mixture evenly over top. Sprinkle remaining dough over fruit. Bake 25 to 30 minutes or until edges and top are lightly browned. Cool completely in pan on wire rack. Cut into bars.

**Prep Time:** 30 minutes

**Bake Time:** 30 minutes

# caribbean crunch shortbread

1 recipe Easy Holiday Shortbread Dough (page 154)

1 cup diced dried tropical fruit, including pineapple, mango and papaya

**Makes about 2 dozen cookies**

1. Prepare Easy Holiday Shortbread Dough, beating in tropical fruit. Shape dough into 14-inch log. Wrap log in plastic wrap; refrigerate 1 hour.

2. Preheat oven to 300°F. Cut log into 1/2-inch-thick slices; place on ungreased cookie sheet. Bake 20 to 25 minutes or until cookies are set and lightly browned. Cool 5 minutes on cookie sheet. Remove cookies to wire rack; cool completely.

# cherry cheesecake bars

1 can (21 ounces) cherry pie filling or topping

2 tablespoons water

1 tablespoon cornstarch

1 package (about 18 ounces) cherry chip or yellow cake mix with pudding in the mix

1/2 cup (1 stick) butter, melted

1 egg

1 container (about 24 ounces) refrigerated ready-to-eat cheesecake filling

1. Place cherry pie filling in medium saucepan. Stir water and cornstarch together in small bowl until cornstarch is dissolved. Stir cornstarch mixture into pie filling until well blended. Bring to a boil over medium heat, stirring constantly. Boil 2 minutes, stirring constantly. Remove from heat; set aside to cool.

2. Preheat oven to 350°F. Spray 13×9-inch baking pan lightly with cooking spray.

3. Combine cake mix, butter and egg in medium bowl until well blended (mixture will be crumbly). Press mixture into bottom of prepared pan. Bake 15 minutes. Cool completely in pan on wire rack.

4. Spread cheesecake filling evenly over cooled crust. Spread cooled cherry topping over cheesecake filling. Cover lightly with plastic wrap; refrigerate at least 4 hours before serving.

**Prep Time:** 25 minutes

**Bake Time:** 15 minutes

**Chill Time:** 4 hours

Makes about 2 dozen bars

# lemon nut white chip cookies

1-1/2 cups all-purpose flour

3/4 teaspoon baking soda

1/2 teaspoon salt

3/4 cup (1-1/2 sticks) butter or margarine, softened

1/2 cup packed brown sugar

1/4 cup granulated sugar

1 egg

1 tablespoon lemon juice

2 cups (12-ounce package) NESTLÉ® TOLL HOUSE®
   Premier White Morsels

1 cup coarsely chopped walnuts or cashew nuts

1 teaspoon grated lemon peel

**PREHEAT** oven to 375°F.

**COMBINE** flour, baking soda and salt in small bowl. Beat butter, brown sugar and granulated sugar in large mixer bowl until creamy. Beat in egg and lemon juice; gradually beat in flour mixture. Stir in morsels, nuts and lemon peel. Drop by rounded tablespoon onto ungreased baking sheets.

**BAKE** for 7 to 10 minutes or until edges are lightly browned. Cool on baking sheets for 3 minutes; remove to wire racks to cool completely.

Makes
about 3 dozen
cookies

# cran-orange oatmeal bars

1/2 cup (1 stick) butter, softened

1/2 cup dried cranberries

1 egg

1 teaspoon grated orange peel, divided

3 tablespoons orange juice, divided

1 package (about 17 ounces) oatmeal cookie mix

1 cup powdered sugar

Makes about 3 dozen bars

1. Preheat oven to 375°F. Spray 13×9-inch baking dish with nonstick cooking spray.

2. Combine butter, cranberries, egg, 1/2 teaspoon orange peel and 1 tablespoon orange juice in medium bowl. Stir in cookie mix until well blended. Spread batter evenly in prepared baking dish.

3. Bake 17 minutes or until light golden brown around edges. Cool completely in pan on wire rack.

4. Blend powdered sugar and remaining 2 tablespoons orange juice in small bowl until smooth. Stir in remaining 1/2 teaspoon orange peel. Drizzle evenly over bars.

# gooey thumbprints

**Makes about 3 dozen cookies**

Easy All-Purpose Cookie Dough (page 152)

1/4 cup strawberry, grape, apricot or favorite flavor jam

1. Prepare and chill cookie dough as directed. Preheat oven to 300°F.

2. Shape dough into 1-inch balls; place 1 inch apart on ungreased cookie sheets. Make small indentation in each ball with thumb; fill with heaping 1/4 teaspoon jam.

3. Bake 25 to 27 minutes or until tops of cookies are light golden brown. Cool 1 minute on cookie sheets. Remove to wire racks; cool completely.

**Variation:** You can also use chocolate hazelnut spread or chocolate spread to fill the cookies instead of jam. Prepare as directed above.

# creamy lemon nut bars

1/2 cup (1 stick) butter or margarine, softened

1/3 cup powdered sugar

2 teaspoons vanilla

1-3/4 cups flour, divided

1/3 cup PLANTERS® Pecans, chopped

1 package (8 ounces) PHILADELPHIA® Cream Cheese, softened

2 cups granulated sugar

3 eggs

1/2 cup lemon juice

1 tablespoon grated lemon peel

1 tablespoon powdered sugar

Makes
32 servings

*To maximize juice yield, roll citrus fruits around on the counter top a few times with your palm before squeezing.*

**PREHEAT** oven to 350°F. Line 13×9-inch baking pan with foil; spray with cooking spray. Mix butter, 1/3 cup powdered sugar and vanilla in large bowl. Gradually stir in 1-1/2 cups of the flour and pecans. Press dough firmly onto bottom of prepared pan. Bake 15 minutes.

**BEAT** cream cheese and granulated sugar in medium bowl with electric mixer on high speed until well blended. Add remaining 1/4 cup flour and eggs; beat until blended.

**STIR** in lemon juice and peel. Pour over baked crust in pan. Bake 30 minutes or until set. Remove from oven; cool completely. Sprinkle with 1 tablespoon powdered sugar; cut into 32 bars.

**How to grate citrus peel:** Always wash and dry citrus fruit before grating. Move whole citrus fruit up and down on the side of the grater with the smallest holes to remove ONLY the surface of the fruit peel. (The inner white part is bitter.) Continue to grate fruit until you have the desired amount of grated peel, rotating fruit on the grater as necessary. Use this technique for grating any citrus fruit.

**Substitute:** Prepare as directed, using lime juice and grated lime peel.

**Prep Time:** 20 minutes plus cooling
**Bake Time:** 30 minutes

Makes
16 servings

Fruit fantasy

# no-bake pineapple marmalade squares

1 cup graham cracker crumbs

1/2 cup plus 2 tablespoons sugar, divided

1/4 cup light margarine, melted

1 cup fat-free or light sour cream

4 ounces light cream cheese, softened

1/4 cup orange marmalade or apricot fruit spread, divided

1 can (20 ounces) DOLE® Crushed Pineapple

1 envelope unflavored gelatin

• Prepare 8-inch square glass baking dish by lining with two sheets of nonstick aluminum foil, placed crosswise in dish.

• Combine graham cracker crumbs, 2 tablespoons sugar and margarine in medium bowl; pat mixture firmly and evenly onto bottom of dish. Freeze 10 minutes.

• Beat sour cream, cream cheese, remaining 1/2 cup sugar and 1 tablespoon marmalade in medium bowl until smooth and blended; set aside.

• Drain crushed pineapple; reserve 1/4 cup juice.

• Sprinkle gelatin over reserved juice in small saucepan; let stand 1 minute. Cook and stir over low heat until gelatin dissolves.

• Beat gelatin mixture into sour cream mixture until well blended. Spoon mixture evenly over crust.

• Stir together crushed pineapple and remaining 3 tablespoons marmalade in small bowl until blended. Evenly spoon over sour cream filling. Cover and refrigerate 2 hours or until firm.

# strawberry & cream cheese fudge brownies

1 package DUNCAN HINES® Family-Style Dark Chocolate Fudge Brownie Mix

1 container DUNCAN HINES® Creamy Home-Style Cream Cheese Frosting

1/4 to 1/2 cup squeezable seedless strawberry jam

**Makes 24 servings**

1. Prepare, bake and cool brownies according to package directions.

2. Spread frosting generously on brownies.

3. Place strawberry jam in resealable plastic food storage bag. Cut one corner off bag and squeeze jam in a zigzag pattern on top of frosting. For decorative effect, run a knife through the jam in opposite directions.

# jammy wedges

1 package (18 ounces) refrigerated
   sugar cookie dough

1/4 cup granulated sugar

1 egg

3 tablespoons blackberry jam

Powdered sugar

Additional blackberry jam
   (optional)

**Makes 8 to 10 servings**

1. Let dough stand at room temperature about 15 minutes. Preheat oven to 350°F. Line bottom of 9-inch glass pie plate with waxed paper. Spray with nonstick cooking spray.

2. Combine dough, granulated sugar and egg in large bowl; beat until well blended. (Dough will be sticky.) Spread dough in prepared pie plate; smooth top. Stir jam in small bowl until smooth. Dot top of dough with jam. Swirl jam into dough using tip of knife.

3. Bake 30 to 35 minutes or until edges are light brown and center is set. Cool 5 minutes in pie plate on wire rack.

4. Sprinkle with powdered sugar and cut into wedges just before serving. Serve with additional jam, if desired.

# orange snickerdoodles

1/2 cup (1 stick) butter, softened

1 cup granulated sugar

1 tablespoon grated orange peel

1 egg

1/2 teaspoon vanilla

1-1/2 cups all-purpose flour

1/4 teaspoon baking soda

1/4 teaspoon cream of tartar

1/4 cup orange-colored sugar*

Icing

1 cup powdered sugar

2 tablespoons orange juice

1/4 teaspoon vanilla

*Granulated sugar may be substituted.

1. Beat butter in large bowl with electric mixer at medium speed 30 seconds. Add granulated sugar and orange peel; beat 1 minute. Beat in egg and vanilla until well blended. Add flour, baking soda and cream of tartar; beat until just combined. (The batter will be very stiff.) Cover with plastic wrap; refrigerate 1 hour.

2. Preheat oven to 375°F. Line cookie sheets with parchment paper.

3. Shape dough into 1-inch balls. Roll balls in orange-colored sugar. Place balls 2 inches apart on prepared cookie sheets. Bake 12 to 15 minutes or until edges are light brown. Cool cookies 5 minutes on cookie sheets.

4. For icing, combine powdered sugar, orange juice and vanilla in small bowl. Whisk until sugar has dissolved, adding more powdered sugar or juice, if desired.

5. Gently loosen cookies from parchment, but leave on sheets. Drizzle icing evenly over warm cookies, using a whisk or fork. Remove to wire racks; cool completely. Store in airtight container.

**Makes
3 dozen cookies**

# Kids' favorites

## spiky pretzel balls

2 cups slightly crushed thin pretzel sticks

1 package (about 18 ounces) carrot or spice cake mix

5 tablespoons butter, melted

2 eggs

1 cup chow mein noodles

1 cup mini semisweet chocolate chips

1 cup butterscotch or peanut butter chips

1. Preheat oven to 350°F. Spray cookie sheets lightly with cooking spray. Place pretzels in shallow bowl.

2. Beat cake mix, butter and eggs in large bowl until well blended. Stir in chow mein noodles, chocolate chips and butterscotch chips. Shape dough into 1-inch balls; roll in pretzel pieces, pressing firmly to adhere.

3. Place 1 inch apart on prepared cookie sheets. Bake 14 minutes or until dough is no longer shiny. Cool 5 minutes on cookie sheets. Remove to wire racks; cool completely. Store leftovers in airtight container.

**Prep Time:** 15 minutes
**Bake Time:** 14 minutes

Makes
about 3 dozen
cookies

# almond brownies

1/2 cup (1 stick) butter

2 squares (1 ounce each) unsweetened baking chocolate

2 eggs

1 cup firmly packed light brown sugar

1/4 teaspoon almond extract

1/2 cup all-purpose flour

1-1/2 cups "M&M's"® Chocolate Mini Baking Bits, divided

1/2 cup slivered almonds, toasted and divided

Chocolate Glaze (recipe follows)

Preheat oven to 350°F. Grease and flour 8×8×2-inch baking pan; set aside. In small saucepan melt butter and chocolate over low heat; stir to blend. Remove from heat; let cool. In medium bowl beat eggs and brown sugar until well blended; stir in chocolate mixture and almond extract. Add flour. Stir in 1 cup "M&M's"® Chocolate Mini Baking Bits and 1/4 cup almonds. Spread batter evenly in prepared pan. Bake 25 to 28 minutes or until firm in center. Cool completely on wire rack. Prepare Chocolate Glaze. Spread over brownies; decorate with remaining 1/2 cup "M&M's"® Chocolate Mini Baking Bits and remaining 1/4 cup almonds. Cut into bars. Store in tightly covered container.

**Chocolate Glaze:** In small saucepan over low heat combine 4 teaspoons water and 1 tablespoon butter until it comes to a boil. Stir in 4 teaspoons unsweetened cocoa powder. Gradually stir in 1/2 cup powdered sugar until smooth. Remove from heat; stir in 1/4 teaspoon vanilla extract. Let glaze cool slightly.

Makes
16 brownies

# happy faces

Easy All-Purpose Cookie Dough (page 152)

Prepared white frosting

Yellow food coloring

Mini and full-size semisweet chocolate chips

Makes 1 to 1-1/2 dozen cookies

1. Prepare and chill cookie dough as directed. Preheat oven to 300°F.

2. Roll out dough to 1/4-inch thickness between two sheets of plastic wrap. Cut out circles with 2-1/2- to 3-inch round cookie cutter. Place 1 inch apart on ungreased cookie sheets.

3. Bake 22 to 27 minutes or until edges are light golden brown. Cool 1 minute on cookie sheets. Remove to wire rack; cool completely.

4. Blend frosting and food coloring in small bowl until desired shade of yellow is reached. Spread thin layer of frosting evenly over cookies. Create faces using chocolate chips for eyes and smiles.

# hot chocolate cookies

1/2 cup (1 stick) butter, softened

1/2 cup sugar

1/4 teaspoon salt

1 cup milk chocolate chips, melted, divided

1 cup all-purpose flour

Mini marshmallows, cut into small pieces

**Makes about 2 dozen cookies**

1. Preheat oven to 350°F. Lightly grease cookie sheets or line with parchment paper.

2. Beat butter, sugar and salt in large bowl with electric mixer at medium speed until well blended. Add 1/4 cup melted chocolate; beat until well blended. Gradually add flour, beating after each addition.

3. Shape dough by level tablespoonfuls into balls. (If dough is too soft, refrigerate 1 hour or until firm enough to handle.) Place 2 inches apart on prepared cookie sheets; flatten to 1/2-inch thickness. Bake 15 to 17 minutes or until set. Cool 5 minutes on cookie sheets. Remove to wire racks; cool completely.

4. Spread about 1 teaspoon remaining melted chocolate onto each cookie. Sprinkle with marshmallow pieces; press gently into chocolate. Refrigerate at least 1 hour or until set.

# peanuts

1/2 cup (1 stick) butter, softened

1/4 cup shortening

1/4 cup creamy peanut butter

1 cup powdered sugar, sifted

1 egg yolk

1 teaspoon vanilla

1-3/4 cups all-purpose flour

1 cup finely ground honey-roasted peanuts, divided

Peanut Buttery Frosting (recipe follows)

Makes
about 2 dozen
cookies

1. Beat butter, shortening and peanut butter in large bowl with electric mixer at medium speed. Gradually add powdered sugar, beating until smooth. Add egg yolk and vanilla; beat well. Add flour; mix well. Stir in 1/3 cup ground peanuts. Cover dough; refrigerate 1 hour. Prepare Peanut Buttery Frosting.

2. Preheat oven to 350°F. Grease cookie sheets. Shape dough into 1-inch balls. Place 2 balls, side by side and slightly touching, on prepared cookie sheet. Gently flatten balls with fingertips to form into "peanut" shape. Repeat steps with remaining dough.

3. Bake 16 to 18 minutes or until edges are lightly browned. Cool 5 minutes on cookie sheets. Remove cookies to wire racks; cool completely.

4. Place remaining 2/3 cup ground peanuts in shallow dish. Spread about 2 teaspoons Peanut Buttery Frosting evenly over top of each cookie. Coat with ground peanuts.

## peanut buttery frosting

1/2 cup (1 stick) butter, softened

1/2 cup creamy peanut butter

2 cups powdered sugar, sifted

1/2 teaspoon vanilla

3 to 6 tablespoons milk

Makes
1-1/2 cups
frosting

Beat butter and peanut butter in medium bowl with electric mixer at medium speed. Gradually add powdered sugar and vanilla until blended but crumbly. Add milk, 1 tablespoon at a time, until smooth. Refrigerate until ready to use.

# chocolate swirl lollipop cookies

1/2 cup (1 stick) butter or margarine, softened

1 cup sugar

2 eggs

1 teaspoon orange extract

1 teaspoon vanilla extract

2-1/4 cups all-purpose flour, divided

1/2 teaspoon baking soda

1/2 teaspoon salt

1/4 teaspoon freshly grated orange peel

Few drops red and yellow food color (optional)

2 sections (1/2 ounce each) HERSHEY'S Unsweetened Chocolate Premium Baking Bar, melted

About 24 wooden popsicle sticks

**Makes about 24 cookies**

*Wrap small cellophane bags around each lollipop cookie with ribbon. These cute gifts make the perfect giveaway for birthday parties.*

1. Beat butter and sugar in large bowl until blended. Add eggs and extracts; beat until light and fluffy. Gradually add 1-1/4 cups flour, blending until smooth. Stir in remaining 1 cup flour, baking soda and salt until mixture is well blended.

2. Place half of batter in medium bowl; stir in orange peel. Stir in food color, if desired. Melt baking chocolate as directed on package; stir into remaining half of batter. Cover; refrigerate both mixtures until firm enough to roll.

3. With rolling pin or fingers, between 2 pieces of wax paper, roll chocolate and orange mixtures each into 10×8-inch rectangle. Remove wax paper; place orange mixture on top of chocolate. Starting on longest side, roll up doughs tightly, forming into 12-inch roll; wrap in plastic wrap. Refrigerate until firm.

4. Heat oven to 350°F. Remove plastic wrap from roll; cut into 1/2-inch-wide slices. Place on cookie sheet at least 3 inches apart. Insert popsicle stick into each cookie.

5. Bake 8 to 10 minutes or until cookie is almost set. Cool slightly; remove from cookie sheet to wire rack. Cool completely. Decorate and tie with ribbon, if desired.

# garbage pail cookies

1 package (about 18 ounces) white cake mix with pudding in the mix

1/2 cup (1 stick) butter, softened

2 eggs

1 teaspoon ground cinnamon

1 teaspoon vanilla

1/2 cup peanut butter chips

1/2 cup salted peanuts

1/2 cup mini candy-coated chocolate pieces

1-1/2 cups crushed salted potato chips

**Makes about 3 dozen cookies**

1. Preheat oven to 350°F. Lightly grease cookie sheets.

2. Beat cake mix, butter, eggs, cinnamon and vanilla in large bowl with electric mixer at medium speed 2 minutes or until well blended. Stir in peanut butter chips, peanuts and candy-coated chocolate pieces. Stir in potato chips. (Dough will be stiff.) Drop batter by rounded tablespoonfuls 2 inches apart onto prepared cookie sheets.

3. Bake 15 minutes or until golden brown. Cool 2 minutes on cookie sheets. Remove to wire racks; cool completely.

# pb&j cookie bars

1 package (about 18 ounces) yellow cake mix with pudding in the mix

1 cup peanut butter

1/2 cup vegetable oil

2 eggs

1 cup strawberry jam

1 cup peanut butter chips

1. Preheat oven to 350°F. Line 15×10-inch jelly-roll pan with foil; spray lightly with cooking spray.

2. Beat cake mix, peanut butter, oil and eggs in large bowl with electric mixer at medium speed until well blended. Press mixture evenly into prepared pan with damp hands. Bake 20 minutes.

3. Place jam in small microwavable bowl; heat on HIGH 20 seconds to soften. Spread jam evenly over cookie base. Scatter peanut butter chips over top.

4. Bake 10 minutes or until edges are browned. Cool completely in pan on wire rack.

**Prep Time:** 20 minutes

**Bake Time:** 30 minutes

Makes about 3 dozen bars

# dinosaur egg cookies

1 cup (2 sticks) margarine or butter, softened

1 cup confectioners' sugar

1 egg

1 teaspoon vanilla

1-1/2 cups all-purpose flour

1-1/4 cups QUAKER® Oats (quick or old fashioned, uncooked)

1/2 cup cornstarch

1/4 teaspoon salt (optional)

24 assorted bite-size candies

Colored sugar or candy sprinkles

**Makes 24 cookies**

1. Heat oven to 325°F. Beat margarine and sugar in large bowl with electric mixer until creamy. Add egg and vanilla; beat well. Combine flour, oats, cornstarch and salt, if desired, in medium bowl; mix well. Add to creamed mixture; mix well.

2. Shape rounded tablespoonfuls of dough into 1-1/2-inch balls. Press candy piece into center of each ball; shape dough around candy so it is completely hidden. Lightly pinch one side of dough to form egg shape. Roll cookies in desired decorations until evenly coated. Place 2 inches apart on ungreased cookie sheets.

3. Bake 16 to 20 minutes or until cookies are set and lightly browned on bottom. Remove to wire rack; cool completely. Store tightly covered.

Make your own colored sugar by combining granulated sugar and a drop of food coloring in a small bowl. Stir well and add additional food coloring until desired shade in reached.

# rocky road crispy treats

6 tablespoons butter

2 packages (10 ounces each) large marshmallows

1 package (12 ounces) semisweet chocolate chips, divided

12 cups crisp rice cereal (13-1/2-ounce box)

1 package (6 ounces) sliced almonds (1-2/3 cups), divided

2 cups mini marshmallows

**Makes 24 to 30 treats**

1. Spray 13×9-inch baking pan with nonstick cooking spray.

2. Melt butter in large saucepan over low heat. Add large marshmallows; stir until completely melted. Stir in 1 cup chocolate chips until melted. Remove pan from heat; stir in cereal until well coated. Add remaining 1 cup chocolate chips, 1 cup almonds and mini marshmallows; stir to distribute evenly.

3. Press mixture firmly into prepared pan with buttered hands to form even layer. Sprinkle with remaining 2/3 cup almonds. Cool completely before cutting. Serve immediately or store in airtight container up to 1 day.

**Prep Time:** 10 minutes
**Cook Time:** 10 minutes

# pot of gold cookies

4-1/2 cups powdered sugar, divided

1 cup (2 sticks) unsalted butter, softened

2 tablespoons packed light brown sugar

1/4 teaspoon salt

2 cups all-purpose flour

6 to 8 tablespoons milk

Yellow sugar

**Makes about 2-1/2 dozen cookies**

1. Beat 1/2 cup powdered sugar, butter, brown sugar and salt in large bowl with electric mixer at medium speed 2 minutes or until light and fluffy. Add flour, 1/2 cup at a time, beating well after each addition.

2. Shape dough into 14-inch-long log. Wrap tightly in plastic wrap; refrigerate 1 hour.

3. Preheat oven to 300°F. Cut log into 1/2-inch-thick slices; place on ungreased cookie sheets. Use scallop-edged cookie cutter to cut slices to resemble coins, if desired. Bake 20 to 25 minutes or until lightly browned. Cool 5 minutes on cookie sheets. Remove to wire racks; cool completely.

4. Place cookies on waxed paper. Combine remaining 4 cups powdered sugar and milk, 1 tablespoon at a time, to make a medium-thick pourable glaze. Spread glaze over cookies and sprinkle with yellow sugar. Let stand 30 minutes to allow glaze to set.

# yellow's nuts for nutty squares

1 cup (2 sticks) plus 2 tablespoons butter, softened and divided

1/2 cup powdered sugar

2-1/4 cups all-purpose flour

1/4 teaspoon salt

3/4 cup granulated sugar

1/2 cup light corn syrup

2 large eggs, beaten

1/2 teaspoon vanilla extract

2 cups coarsely chopped mixed nuts

1 cup "M&M's"® Semi-Sweet Chocolate Mini Baking Bits

Preheat oven to 325°F. Lightly grease 13×9-inch baking pan; set aside. In large bowl beat 1 cup (2 sticks) butter and powdered sugar; gradually add flour and salt until well blended. Press dough evenly onto bottom and 1/2 inch up sides of prepared pan. Bake 25 to 30 minutes or until very light golden brown. In small saucepan melt remaining 2 tablespoons butter; let cool slightly. In large bowl combine melted butter, granulated sugar, corn syrup, eggs and vanilla. Pour filling over partially baked crust; sprinkle with nuts and "M&M's"® Semi-Sweet Chocolate Mini Baking Bits. Return to oven; bake 30 to 35 minutes or until filling is set. Remove pan to wire rack; cool completely. Cut into bars. Store in tightly covered container.

Makes
2 dozen bars

# s'more brownies

1 package (19-1/2 ounces) brownie mix

2 eggs

1/2 cup vegetable oil

1/4 cup water

1 jar (7-1/2 ounces) marshmallow crème

12 graham crackers

**Makes 12 brownies**

1. Preheat oven to 350°F. Grease 13×9-inch baking pan or coat with nonstick cooking spray.

2. Combine brownie mix, eggs, oil and water in large bowl. Pour into prepared pan. Bake 25 minutes or until set in center. Cool 10 minutes in pan. Spread marshmallow evenly over brownies. Let stand 5 minutes.

3. Break graham crackers in half to form squares. Place layer of crackers on top of marshmallow layer. Cut around graham squares. Carefully remove brownies from pan. Place cracker square underneath each brownie. Press to adhere. Serve warm.

# chocolate peanut butter swirls

1 recipe Basic Short Dough (page 150)

3 tablespoons peanut butter

1 recipe Basic Chocolate Short Dough (page 150)

1 egg white

1 tablespoon water

**Makes 4 dozen cookies**

1. Prepare Basic Short Dough, adding peanut butter with the egg yolks. Divide dough in half. On lightly floured surface, roll out each dough half into 8-inch square. Cover with plastic wrap; set aside.

2. Prepare Basic Chocolate Short Dough. Divide dough in half. On lightly floured surface, roll out each dough half into 8-inch square. Mix egg white with 1 tablespoon water; blend well. Brush egg wash on top of both chocolate dough squares. Place each peanut butter dough square on top of each chocolate square. Roll up jelly-roll fashion to just short of center. Turn dough over and roll other half to center, forming "S" shape. Wrap each roll in plastic wrap. Refrigerate at least 2 hours or overnight.

3. Preheat oven to 375°F. Line cookie sheets with parchment paper. Cut logs into 1/4-inch-thick slices. Place cookies 1 inch apart on cookie sheets. Bake 14 to 16 minutes or until firm. Cool cookies 5 minutes on cookie sheets. Remove to wire racks; cool completely. Store in airtight container.

1 recipe Basic Gingerbread Dough (page 151)

Light corn syrup

1 package (about 17 ounces) multi-colored rolled fondant, divided

Supplies
Cookie cutters
Pastry brush
Sharp knife
Rolling cutter, straight or wavy

Makes about 2 dozen cookies

1. Preheat oven to 350°F. Line several cookie sheets with parchment paper.

2. Prepare gingerbread dough. Roll out warm dough to 1/4-inch thickness. Cut out desired quantity of mittens, caps and scarfs, using cookie cutters or stencils. Re-roll dough scraps once. Place cookies 2 inches apart on prepared sheets. Bake 15 to 18 minutes or until lightly browned. Cool cookies 5 minutes on cookie sheets. Remove to wire racks; cool completely.

3. Decorate as desired. Store in airtight container. If cookies are intended for decoration only, they will keep for several weeks.

**Cap & Scarf Cookies:** Roll out desired colors of fondant into 1/8-inch-thick rectangle. Keep fondant covered with plastic wrap at all times to prevent drying out. Using rolling cutter, cut each color fondant rectangle into 1/4-inch strips. Lay strips of fondant side by side, alternating colors. Lightly roll striped fondant with rolling pin to join pieces together. Using same cookie cutter or stencils used for cookies, cut out pieces of striped fondant. Place a small amount of corn syrup in small bowl. Using pastry brush, spread thin layer of corn syrup onto baked cookies. Lay cut pieces of fondant directly onto cookies. Press down to adhere. Run your hands across the fondant to smooth and connect the strips. For cap top, roll desired color fondant into 1-inch ball. Use small scissors to make cuts into ball. Press ball at top of cap, using corn syrup to adhere to cookie. For fringe on scarf, roll desired color fondant 1/8 inch thick. Cut into 1/2-inch squares. Remember to create 2 sets of fringe for each scarf cookie. Using a small paring knife, cut tiny strips across the rectangle just up to the top, leaving strips connected at top. Brush ends of scarf cookie with corn syrup. Lay fringes on each end of scarfs. Press down to adhere.

**Mitten Cookies:** Roll out desired color of fondant to 1/8-inch thickness. Using mitten cookie cutter or stencil, cut out pieces of fondant. Cut out small circles in fondant. Replace cut circles with various colors of fondant, using same cutter. Spread thin layer of corn syrup on cookies; lay cut pieces of fondant directly onto cookies. Press down to adhere. Run your hands across the fondant to smooth.

1 cup (2 sticks) butter or margarine, softened

1-1/3 cups granulated sugar

2 egg yolks

1/4 cup milk

2 teaspoons vanilla extract

2 cups all-purpose flour

2/3 cup HERSHEY'S Cocoa

1/2 teaspoon salt

Powdered sugar

1 can (16 ounces) vanilla frosting

Additional powdered sugar

1-1/3 cups (10.5-ounce package) HERSHEY'S KISSABLES Chocolate Candies

**Makes about 3-1/2 dozen cookies**

1. Beat butter, granulated sugar, egg yolks, milk and vanilla until fluffy. Combine flour, cocoa and salt; gradually add to butter mixture, beating until well blended. Cover; refrigerate dough about 2 hours or until firm enough to handle.

2. Heat oven to 350°F. Lightly grease cookie sheet. Shape dough into 1-1/8-inch balls. Roll in powdered sugar; place on prepared cookie sheet. Press thumb into center of each cookie.

3. Bake 10 to 12 minutes or until set. Remove from cookie sheet to wire rack; cool completely.

4. Spoon frosting into heavy-duty resealable plastic food storage bag. Cut off corner of bag about 1/4 inch from point; pipe frosting into thumbprint indentations. Sift additional powdered sugar over filled cookies, if desired. Gently press 3 to 4 candies into each filled cookie.

**Vanilla Variation:** Increase flour to 2-3/4 cups; omit cocoa.

# Seasonal treats

## white chocolate shamrocks

2 packages (18 ounces each) refrigerated sugar cookie dough

1/2 cup all-purpose flour

Green food coloring

1 package (14 ounces) white candy melting disks

Green sprinkles, dragées or colored sugar

Makes about 2 dozen cookies

1. Let dough stand at room temperature 15 minutes. Preheat oven to 350°F. Lightly grease cookie sheets.

2. Beat dough, flour and enough food coloring until desired color of green is reached. Divide dough in half; refrigerate one half.

3. Roll half of dough to 1/4-inch thickness. Cut shamrock shapes using cookie cutter or stencil. Place 2 inches apart onto prepared cookie sheets. Repeat with remaining dough.

4. Bake 8 to 10 minutes or until set. Cool 5 minutes on cookie sheets. Remove to wire racks; cool completely.

5. Melt candy disks according to package directions; whisk until smooth. Dip one edge of each cookie into melted chocolate; decorate as desired. Place on waxed paper until set.

# super-lucky cereal treats

40 large marshmallows

1/4 cup (1/2 stick) butter

6 cups oat cereal with marshmallow bits

Irish-themed candy cake decorations

**Makes 16 treats**

1. Line 8-inch square pan with foil, leaving 2-inch overhang on 2 sides. Generously grease or spray with nonstick cooking spray.

2. Melt marshmallows and butter in medium saucepan over medium heat 3 minutes or until melted and smooth, stirring constantly. Remove from heat.

3. Add cereal; stir until completely coated. Spread into prepared pan; press evenly onto bottom using rubber spatula. Let cool 10 minutes. Remove treats from pan using foil. Cut into 16 bars. Press candy decorations onto top of treats while still warm.

# fudgey nut passover brownies

1/2 cup (1 stick) butter

2 eggs

1 cup sugar

1/4 cup HERSHEY'S Cocoa

1/2 cup matzo cake meal

1/2 cup slivered almonds, toasted and chopped*

Fresh strawberries (optional)

*To toast almonds: Heat oven to 350°F. Spread almonds in thin layer in shallow baking pan. Bake 8 to 10 minutes, stirring occasionally, until light golden brown. Cool completely.

**Makes 16 brownies**

1. Heat oven to 325°F. Line 8-inch square baking pan with foil; lightly butter foil.

2. Melt butter; set aside to cool slightly. Using spoon, beat eggs lightly in medium bowl. Add sugar; beat well. Stir in cocoa and melted butter until well blended. Stir in matzo cake meal, then chopped nuts. Pour into prepared pan.

3. Bake 25 to 30 minutes or until brownie is set and surface is shiny. Cool completely in pan on wire rack. Remove from pan; remove and discard foil. Cut into squares. Garnish serving plate with strawberries, if desired.

# festive easter cookies

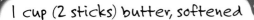

1 cup (2 sticks) butter, softened

2 cups powdered sugar

1 egg

2 teaspoons grated lemon peel

1 teaspoon vanilla

3 cups all-purpose flour

1/2 teaspoon salt

Royal Icing (page 153)

Assorted food colorings

Assorted sprinkles and candies

When rolling out cookie dough, always start at the center and roll outward. To prevent sticking, spray work surface and rolling pin with nonstick cooking spray.

1. Beat butter and powdered sugar in large bowl with electric mixer at high speed until fluffy. Add egg, lemon peel and vanilla; beat well. Combine flour and salt in medium bowl. Add to butter mixture; mix well.

2. Divide dough in half. Wrap each half in plastic wrap. Refrigerate 3 hours or overnight.

3. Preheat oven to 375°F. Roll dough on floured surface to 1/8-inch thickness. Cut out dough using Easter cookie cutters, such as eggs, bunnies and tulips. Place cutouts on ungreased cookie sheets.

4. Bake 8 to 12 minutes or just until edges are very lightly browned. Remove to wire racks; cool completely. Prepare Royal Icing; tint with food colorings as desired. Decorate cookies with icing, sprinkles and candies.

Makes 4 dozen
cookies

# tombstone brownies

1 package (21.5 ounces) brownie mix plus ingredients to prepare mix

1 cup chocolate fudge frosting (about 1/2 of 16-ounce container)

2 milk chocolate candy bars (1.5 ounces each)

Creamy Decorator's Frosting (page 154)

3/4 cup shredded coconut, tinted green (see note)

12 pumpkin candies

**Makes 12 servings**

1. Preheat oven to 350°F. Line 13×9-inch baking pan with foil, leaving 2-inch overhang on 2 sides; grease foil.

2. Prepare brownie mix according to package directions. Spread in prepared pan. Bake 30 to 35 minutes. *Do not overbake.* Cool in pan on wire rack.

3. Using foil as handles, remove brownies from pan; peel off foil. Frost with chocolate frosting. Cut brownies into twelve 4×2-inch bars.

4. Break each chocolate bar into 6 pieces along scored lines. Write "R.I.P." on chocolate pieces using Creamy Decorator's Frosting. Let stand until set.

5. Press 1 chocolate piece into end of each brownie for tombstone. Sprinkle tinted coconut on each brownie for grass. Place 1 pumpkin candy on coconut.

**Note:** To tint coconut, dilute a few drops of food coloring with 1/2 teaspoon water in a large plastic bag. Add shredded coconut. Close the bag and shake well until the coconut is evenly coated. If a deeper color is desired, add more diluted food coloring and shake again.

# chunky pecan pie bars

## Crust

1-1/2 cups all-purpose flour

1/2 cup (1 stick) butter or margarine, softened

1/4 cup packed brown sugar

## Filling

3 eggs

3/4 cup corn syrup

3/4 cup granulated sugar

2 tablespoons butter or margarine, melted

1 teaspoon vanilla extract

1-3/4 cups (11.5-ounce package) NESTLÉ® TOLL HOUSE® Semi-Sweet Chocolate Chunks

1-1/2 cups coarsely chopped pecans

Makes
2 to 3 dozen
bars

**PREHEAT** oven to 350°F. Grease 13×9-inch baking pan.

**For Crust**
**BEAT** flour, butter and brown sugar in small mixer bowl until crumbly. Press into prepared baking pan.

**BAKE** for 12 to 15 minutes or until lightly browned.

**For Filling**
**BEAT** eggs, corn syrup, granulated sugar, butter and vanilla extract in medium bowl with wire whisk. Stir in chunks and nuts. Pour evenly over baked crust.

**BAKE** for 25 to 30 minutes or until set. Cool completely in pan on wire rack. Cut into bars.

Baked goods that contain corn syrup will retain their moisture better and will stay fresh longer.

# hanukkah cookies

1/2 cup (1 stick) unsalted butter, softened

1/2 cup sugar

1 package (3 ounces) cream cheese

1/4 cup honey

1 egg

1/2 teaspoon vanilla

2-1/2 cups all-purpose flour

1/3 cup finely ground walnuts

1 teaspoon baking powder

1/4 teaspoon salt

Blue, white and yellow decorating icings

**Makes 3-1/2 dozen cookies**

1. Beat butter, sugar, cream cheese, honey, egg and vanilla in large bowl with electric mixer at medium speed until creamy. Stir in flour, walnuts, baking powder and salt until well blended. Form dough into ball; wrap in plastic wrap and flatten. Refrigerate about 2 hours or until firm.

2. Preheat oven to 350°F. Lightly grease cookie sheets. Roll out dough, working with one small portion at a time, to 1/4-inch thickness on floured surface with lightly floured rolling pin. (Keep remaining dough wrapped in refrigerator.) Cut dough with 2-1/2-inch dreidel and 6-pointed star cookie cutters. Place 2 inches apart onto prepared cookie sheets.

3. Bake 8 to 10 minutes or until edges are lightly browned. Cool cookies 1 to 2 minutes on cookie sheets. Remove to wire racks; cool completely. Decorate as desired with blue, white and yellow icings.

# ginger shortbread delights

1 cup (2 sticks) unsalted butter, softened

1/2 cup powdered sugar

1/3 cup packed light brown sugar

1/2 teaspoon salt

2 cups minus 2 tablespoons all-purpose flour

4 ounces crystallized ginger

Bittersweet Glaze (recipe follows)

**Makes about 3-1/2 dozen cookies**

1. Preheat oven to 300°F.

2. Beat butter, sugars and salt in large bowl with electric mixer at medium speed until creamy. Gradually add flour, beating until well blended.

3. Shape dough by tablespoons into balls. Place 1 inch apart on ungreased cookie sheets; flatten to 1/2-inch thickness. Cut ginger into 1/4-inch-thick slices. Place 1 slice ginger on top of each cookie.

4. Bake 20 minutes or until set and lightly browned. Cool 5 minutes on cookie sheets. Remove to wire racks; cool completely.

5. Prepare Bittersweet Glaze; drizzle over cookies. Let stand about 30 minutes or until glaze is set.

*Fans of ginger will love the flavor of these cookies, but they're just as tasty without the crystallized ginger. For another option, before baking, place a pecan or walnut half in the center of each dough ball, or roll them in chopped almonds, hazelnuts or macadamia nuts.*

## bittersweet glaze

1 bar (3 to 3-1/2 ounces) bittersweet chocolate, broken into small pieces

2 tablespoons unsalted butter

2 tablespoons whipping cream

1 tablespoon powdered sugar

1/8 teaspoon salt

Melt chocolate and butter in top of double boiler over hot, not boiling, water. Remove from heat. Add cream, powdered sugar and salt; stir until smooth.

# philadelphia® snowmen cookies

1 package (8 ounces) PHILADELPHIA® Cream Cheese, softened

1 cup powdered sugar

3/4 cup (1-1/2 sticks) butter or margarine

1/2 teaspoon vanilla

2 cups flour

1/2 teaspoon baking soda

Suggested decorations, such as decorating gels, colored sprinkles, nonpareils and peanut butter cups

**Makes about 3 dozen cookies**

**MIX** cream cheese, sugar, butter and vanilla with electric mixer on medium speed until well blended. Add flour and baking soda; mix well.

**SHAPE** dough into equal number of 1/2-inch and 1-inch diameter balls. Using 1 small and 1 large ball for each snowman, place balls, slightly overlapping, on ungreased cookie sheet. Flatten to 1/4-inch thickness with bottom of glass dipped in additional flour. Repeat with remaining dough.

**BAKE** at 325°F for 19 to 21 minutes or until lightly browned. Cool on wire rack. Sprinkle each snowman with sifted powdered sugar. Decorate with decorating gels, colored sprinkles and nonpareils to resemble snowmen. Place 1 candy half on top of each snowman for hats.

**Take a Shortcut:** To speed-soften cream cheese, unwrap and microwave on HIGH for 10 to 15 seconds.

**Prep Time:** 20 minutes

**Total Time:** 41 minutes

# jingle bells ice cream sandwiches

1 package (about 18 ounces) devil's food cake mix

5 tablespoons butter or margarine, melted

3 eggs

50 hard peppermint candies, unwrapped

1 quart vanilla ice cream

1. Preheat oven to 350°F. Spray cookie sheets lightly with nonstick cooking spray.

2. Beat cake mix, butter and eggs in large bowl with electric mixer at medium speed 1 to 2 minutes or until blended and smooth. Drop dough by rounded tablespoons 2 inches apart on prepared cookie sheets. Bake 12 minutes or until edges are set and centers are no longer shiny. Cool 5 minutes on cookie sheet. Remove to wire rack; cool completely.

3. Place peppermint candies in medium resealable food storage bag. Seal bag; crush candies with rolling pin or back of small skillet. Place crushed candies in small bowl. Line shallow pan with waxed paper.

4. Place scoop of ice cream onto flat side of one cookie. Top with a second cookie; roll edge of ice cream in crushed peppermints. Place on shallow pan. Repeat with remaining ice cream, cookies and peppermints. Cover pan; freeze until serving time.

**Prep Time:** 25 minutes

**Bake Time:** 12 minutes

Makes about
1-1/2 dozen
sandwiches

# pink peppermint meringues

3 egg whites

1/8 teaspoon peppermint extract

5 drops red food coloring

1/2 cup superfine sugar*

6 hard peppermint candies, finely crushed

*Or use 1/2 cup granulated sugar processed in food processor 1 minute until very fine.*

**Makes about 6 dozen meringues**

1. Preheat oven to 200°F. Line cookie sheets with parchment paper.

2. Beat egg whites in medium bowl with electric mixer at medium-high speed 45 seconds or until frothy. Beat in peppermint extract and food coloring. Add sugar, 1 tablespoon at a time, while mixer is running. Beat until egg whites are stiff and glossy.

3. Drop meringue by teaspoonfuls into 1-inch mounds on prepared cookie sheets; sprinkle evenly with crushed candies.

4. Bake 2 hours or until meringues are dry when tapped. Transfer parchment paper with meringues to wire racks; cool completely.

# christmas lights and ornament cookies

1 recipe Basic Short Dough (page 150)

1 recipe Royal Icing (page 153)

Assorted food colorings

White dragées

Decorating sugars and edible glitters, various colors

Assorted food colorings

Supplies

Ornament cookie cutters

Plastic straw

Various ribbons

Makes
2 dozen cookies

1. Preheat oven to 350°F. Line cookie sheets with parchment paper.

2. Prepare Basic Short Dough and refrigerate as directed. On lightly floured work surface, roll out dough to 1/4-inch thickness. Cut out ornaments and lights with cutters or stencils. Re-roll dough scraps once. Place 1 inch apart on prepared sheets. Using plastic straw, punch hole at the top of each cookie, about 1/4 inch from edge. Bake 12 to 15 minutes or until golden brown. Cool cookies 5 minutes on cookie sheets. Remove to wire racks; cool completely.

3. Prepare Royal Icing. Thin with water to soft, spreadable consistency. Divide icing into as many small bowls as desired colors. Keep all icings covered with damp paper towels. Decorate as desired.

4. To hang cookies, cut pieces of ribbon to desired length. Slip ribbon through hole and make a small knot.

5. Store cookies in airtight container. If cookies are strictly for decoration, they will keep for several weeks.

**Christmas Lights Cookies:** Spread thin layer of white icing on cookie, just to edge. Before icing sets, sprinkle top half with gold sugar. Sprinkle bottom half of cookie with red or blue edible glitter. Push plastic straw through hole in cookie to remove any icing before it sets. Let cookies dry completely.

**Christmas Ornament:** Spread thin layer of white icing on cookie, just to edge. Before icing sets, place dragées around edge and sprinkle with white edible glitter. Let cookies dry completely.

**Variation:** Basic Gingerbread Dough (page 151) may be substituted for Basic Short Dough.

# santa's favorite brownies

1 cup (6 ounces) milk chocolate chips

1/2 cup (1 stick) butter

3/4 cup granulated sugar

2 eggs

1 teaspoon vanilla

1-1/4 cups all-purpose flour

3 tablespoons unsweetened cocoa powder

1 teaspoon baking powder

1/2 teaspoon salt

1/2 cup chopped walnuts

Buttercream Frosting (page 153)

Sprinkles, decorating icing gels and colored sugar for decoration (optional)

**Makes about 1 dozen brownies**

1. Preheat oven to 350°F. Grease 9-inch square baking pan.

2. Melt chocolate chips, butter and granulated sugar in medium saucepan over low heat, stirring constantly. Pour into large bowl.

3. Add eggs and vanilla to chocolate mixture; beat with electric mixer at medium speed until well blended. Stir in flour, cocoa, baking powder and salt; blend well. Stir in walnuts. Spread in prepared pan.

4. Bake 25 to 30 minutes or until center is firm to the touch. Cool completely in pan on wire rack.

5. Frost with Buttercream Frosting. Cut into bars. Decorate as desired. Store in airtight container.

# Doughs & icings

## basic oatmeal dough

2 1/4 cup uncooked old-fashioned oats
1-1/3 cups all-purpose flour
3/4 teaspoon baking soda
1/2 teaspoon baking powder
1/2 teaspoon salt
1 cup packed light brown sugar
3/4 cup (1-1/2 sticks) butter, softened
1/4 cup granulated sugar
1 egg
1 tablespoon honey
1 teaspoon vanilla

Makes 3 dozen cookies

Combine oats, flour, baking soda, baking powder and salt in medium bowl. Beat brown sugar, butter and granulated sugar in large bowl with electric mixer at medium speed until light and fluffy. Add egg, honey and vanilla; beat until well blended. Gradually add flour mixture, about 1/2 cup at a time; beat just until blended.

**Baking Directions:** Preheat oven to 350°F. Line cookie sheets with parchment paper. Drop dough by tablespoonfuls about 2 inches apart onto prepared cookie sheets. Bake 11 to 15 minutes or until cookies are puffed and golden. *Do not overbake.* Cool 5 minutes on cookie sheets. Remove to wire racks; cool completely.

# basic short dough

3/4 cup (1-1/2 sticks) butter, slightly softened

3/4 cup sugar

3 egg yolks

1 teaspoon vanilla

2 cups all-purpose flour

1/4 teaspoon salt

Beat butter and sugar in large bowl with electric mixer at medium speed 1 minute. Beat in egg yolks and vanilla until well blended. Scrape down bowl. Add flour and salt all at once; mix until just combined. Use immediately according to selected recipe or shape into 2 discs; wrap in plastic wrap and refrigerate. Dough will keep in refrigerator up to 3 days, or in freezer up to 1 month.

**Basic Chocolate Short Dough:** Reduce all-purpose flour to 1-1/2 cups and add 1/2 cup unsweetened cocoa powder. Follow directions above.

# basic gingerbread dough

5 cups all-purpose flour

1 tablespoon ground ginger

2 teaspoons ground cinnamon

1 teaspoon salt

1 cup shortening

1 cup granulated sugar

1 cup molasses

1. Sift together flour, ginger, cinnamon and salt in medium bowl; set aside. Combine shortening, sugar and molasses in medium saucepan. Stir over low heat until shortening melts. Remove from heat; pour into large mixing bowl. Let cool 5 minutes.

2. Add flour mixture to warm molasses mixture. Beat with electric mixer at low speed just until a dough forms. The dough should be somewhat soft, but not sticky. Add more flour as needed. Let dough rest 5 minutes. Roll warm dough as directed by selected recipe.

# easy all-purpose cookie dough

1 cup (2 sticks) butter, softened

1/2 cup powdered sugar

2 tablespoons packed light brown sugar

1/4 teaspoon salt

1 egg

2 cups all-purpose flour

1. Beat butter, powdered sugar, brown sugar and salt in large bowl with electric mixer at medium speed 2 minutes or until light and fluffy. Add egg; beat until well blended.

2. Add flour, 1/2 cup at a time, beating well after each addition. Shape dough into disc; wrap tightly in plastic wrap. Refrigerate at least 1 hour or until firm.

# royal icing

1 egg white,* at room temperature

2 to 2-1/2 cups sifted powdered sugar

1/2 teaspoon almond extract

*Use only grade A clean, uncracked egg.*

1. Beat egg white in small bowl with electric mixer at high speed until foamy.

2. Gradually add 2 cups powdered sugar and almond extract. Beat at low speed until moistened. Increase mixer speed to high and beat until icing is stiff, adding additional powdered sugar if needed.

# buttercream frosting

3 cups powdered sugar, sifted

1/2 cup (1 stick) butter, softened

3 to 4 tablespoons milk, divided

1/2 teaspoon vanilla

Makes about 1-1/2 cups frosting

Combine powdered sugar, butter, 2 tablespoons milk and vanilla in large bowl. Beat with electric mixer at low speed until blended. Beat at high speed until light and fluffy, adding more milk, 1 teaspoon at a time, to reach good spreading consistency.

# easy holiday shortbread dough

1 cup (2 sticks) unsalted butter, softened

1/2 cup powdered sugar

2 tablespoons packed light brown sugar

1/4 teaspoon salt

2 cups all-purpose flour

Beat butter, powdered sugar, brown sugar and salt in large bowl with electric mixer at medium speed 2 minutes or until light and fluffy. Add flour, 1/2 cup at a time, beating well after each addition. Shape dough into 14-inch-long log. Wrap tightly in plastic wrap; refrigerate 1 hour.

**Baking Directions:** Preheat oven to 300°F. Cut log into 1/2-inch-thick slices; place on ungreased cookie sheets. Bake 20 to 25 minutes or until lightly browned. Cool 5 minutes on cookie sheets. Remove to wire racks; cool completely.

# creamy decorator's frosting

1-1/2 cups shortening

1-1/2 teaspoons lemon, coconut, almond or peppermint extract

7-1/2 cups sifted powdered sugar

1/3 cup milk

Makes about 5 cups

Beat shortening and extract in large bowl with electric mixer at medium speed until fluffy. Slowly add half of sugar, 1/2 cup at a time, beating well after each addition. Beat in milk and remaining sugar. Beat one minute more or until smooth and fluffy.* Store in refrigerator. (Frosting may be used for frosting cake and/or piping decorations.)

*If frosting seems too soft for piping roses or other detailed flowers or borders, refrigerate for a few hours. Refrigerating frosting usually gives better results, but you may also try stirring in additional sifted sugar, 1/4 cup at a time, until desired consistency.

**The publisher would like to thank the companies listed below for the use of their recipes in this publication.**

ACH Food Companies, Inc.

Dole Food Company, Inc.

Duncan Hines® and Moist Deluxe® are registered trademarks of Pinnacle Foods Corp.

EAGLE BRAND®

The Hershey Company

©2009 Kraft Foods, KRAFT, KRAFT Hexagon Logo, PHILADELPHIA AND PHILADELPHIA Logo are registered trademarks of Kraft Foods Holdings, Inc. All rights reserved.

© Mars, Incorporated 2009

Mott's® is a registered trademark of Mott's, LLP

Nestlé USA

The Quaker® Oatmeal Kitchens

## A

Almond Brownies, 104
Almond Shortbread Cookies with Chocolate Filling, 56
Apricot Shortbread Diamonds, 82
Aztec Brownies, 38

## B

Basic Chocolate Short Dough, 150
Basic Gingerbread Dough, 151
Basic Oatmeal Dough, 149
Basic Short Dough, 150
**Bittersweet Chocolate**
    Bittersweet Glaze, 139
    Chocolate-Frosted Lebkuchen, 30
    Ginger Shortbread Delights, 138
Bittersweet Glaze, 139
Black Forest Bars, 68
**Brownie Mix**
    Philadelphia® Cheesecake Brownies, 74
    S'more Brownies, 120
    Strawberry & Cream Cheese Fudge Brownies, 98
    Tombstone Brownies, 133
Buttercream Frosting, 153
Butterscotch Toffee Gingersnap Squares, 24

## C

**Cake Mix**
    Apricot Shortbread Diamonds, 82
    Black Forest Bars, 68
    Cherry Cheesecake Bars, 89
    Chinese Almond Cookies, 33
    Chocolate and Oat Toffee Bars, 12
    Cobbled Fruit Bars, 87
    Coconut Key Lime Bars, 77
    Garbage Pail Cookies, 112
    Jingle Bells Ice Cream Sandwiches, 142
    PB&J Cookie Bars, 113
    Peanut Butter Toffee Chewies, 5
    Red Velvet Brownies, 10
    Spiky Pretzel Balls, 103
    Whoppie Pies, 8

Caramel-Kissed Pecan Cookies, 14
Caribbean Crunch Shortbread, 88
**Cherries**
    Black Forest Bars, 68
    Cherry Cheesecake Bars, 89
    Cobbled Fruit Bars, 87
    Danish Cookie Rings (Vanillekranser), 37
    Double Chocolate Cherry Cookies, 80
Cherry Cheesecake Bars, 89
Chewy Brown Butter Pine Nut Triangles, 34
Chewy Peanut Butter Brownies, 60
Chinese Almond Cookies, 33
Chocolate 'n' Oat Bars, 61
Chocolate and Oat Toffee Bars, 12
Chocolate Chunk Cookies, 26
Chocolate Filling, 57
Chocolate-Frosted Lebkuchen, 30
Chocolate Glaze, 104
Chocolate Hazelnut Wedges, 44
Chocolate Oat Shortbread, 69
Chocolate Peanut Butter Swirls, 121
Chocolate Spritz, 75
Chocolate Swirl Lollipop Cookies, 110
Christmas Lights and Ornament Cookies, 144
Chunky Double Chocolate Cookies, 62
Chunky Pecan Pie Bars, 134
Classic Layer Bars, 16
Cobbled Fruit Bars, 87
Cocoa Raisin-Chip Cookies, 53
**Coconut**
    Classic Layer Bars, 16
    Coconut Almond Biscotti, 46
    Coconut Key Lime Bars, 77
    Double Chocolate Coconut Oatmeal Cookies, 58
    Piña Colada Cookie Bars, 83
    Tombstone Brownies, 133
Cran-Orange Oatmeal Bars, 92
Creamy Decorator's Frosting, 154
Creamy Lemon Nut Bars, 94
Crispy Toffee Cookies, 19

## D

Danish Cookie Rings (Vanillekranser), 37
Dinosaur Egg Cookies, 114
Double Chocolate Cherry Cookies, 80
Double Chocolate Coconut Oatmeal Cookies, 58
Double Chocolate Pecan Cookies, 81
Double Striped Peanut Butter Oatmeal Cookies, 22
**Dried Fruit**
  Apricot Shortbread Diamonds, 82
  Caribbean Crunch Shortbread, 88
  Cobbled Fruit Bars, 87
  Cocoa Raisin-Chip Cookies, 53
  Cran-Orange Oatmeal Bars, 92
  Irish Soda Bread Cookies, 40
Dulce de Leche Blondies, 32

## E

Easy All-Purpose Cookie Dough, 152
Easy Holiday Shortbread Cookies, 154
English Toffee Bars, 29
Extra-Chocolatey Brownie Cookies, 70

## F

Festive Easter Cookies, 130
Finnish Nut Logs (Pahkinaleivat), 42
Fudgey Nut Passover Brownies, 129

## G

Garbage Pail Cookies, 112
Ginger Shortbread Delights, 138
Gingersnaps, 11
Gooey Thumbprints, 93
**Graham Crackers**
  Classic Layer Bars, 16
  No-Bake Pineapple Marmalade Squares, 97
  Oatmeal S'mores Cookies, 66
  Piña Colada Cookie Bars, 83
  S'more Brownies, 120

## H

Hanukkah Cookies, 136
Happy Faces, 106

Hot Chocolate Cookies, 107

## I

Irish Flag Cookies, 51
Irish Soda Bread Cookies, 40

## J

Jammy Wedges, 99
Jingle Bells Ice Cream Sandwiches, 142

## K

Kissables Chocolate Candies Thumbprint Cookies, 124

## L

**Lemon**
  Chocolate-Frosted Lebkuchen, 30
  Creamy Lemon Nut Bars, 94
  Lemon Nut White Chip Cookies, 90

## M

**Marshmallow**
  Hot Chocolate Cookies, 107
  Oatmeal S'mores Cookies, 66
  Rocky Road Crispy Treats, 116
  S'more Brownies, 120
  Super-Lucky Cereal Treats, 128
  Whoppie Pies, 8
**Milk Chocolate**
  Almond Shortbread Cookies with Chocolate Filling, 56
  Butterscotch Toffee Gingersnap Squares, 24
  Caramel-Kissed Pecan Cookies, 14
  Chocolate Filling, 57
  Double Striped Peanut Butter Oatmeal Cookies, 22
  English Toffee Bars, 29
  Hot Chocolate Cookies, 107
  Peanut Butter Crème Blossoms, 65
  Peanut Butter Toffee Chewies, 5
  Santa's Favorite Brownies, 146
  Tombstone Brownies, 133
Mississippi Mud Bars, 21
Mitten, Cap and Scarf Cookies, 122
Molded Scottish Shortbread, 41

# N

No-Bake Pineapple Marmalade Squares, 97
Norwegian Almond Squares, 48

**Nuts**

Almond Brownies, 104
Almond Shortbread Cookies with Chocolate Filling, 56
Apricot Shortbread Diamonds, 82
Aztec Brownies, 38
Black Forest Bars, 68
Butterscotch Toffee Gingersnap Squares, 24
Caramel-Kissed Pecan Cookies, 14
Chewy Brown Butter Pine Nut Triangles, 34
Chinese Almond Cookies, 33
Chocolate 'n' Oat Bars, 61
Chocolate and Oat Toffee Bars, 12
Chocolate Chunk Cookies, 26
Chocolate-Frosted Lebkuchen, 30
Chocolate Hazelnut Wedges, 44
Chunky Pecan Pie Bars, 134
Classic Layer Bars, 16
Cocoa Raisin-Chip Cookies, 53
Coconut Almond Biscotti, 46
Creamy Lemon Nut Bars, 94
Crispy Toffee Cookies, 19
Danish Cookie Rings (Vanillekranser), 37
Double Chocolate Coconut Oatmeal Cookies, 58
Double Chocolate Pecan Cookies, 81
English Toffee Bars, 29
Extra-Chocolatey Brownie Cookies, 70
Finnish Nut Logs (Pahkinaleivat), 42
Fudgey Nut Passover Brownies, 129
Garbage Pail Cookies, 112
Lemon Nut White Chip Cookies, 90
Mississippi Mud Bars, 21
Norwegian Almond Squares, 48
Original Nestlé® Toll House® Chocolate Chip Cookies, 72
Parmesan Pine Nut Shortbread, 49
Peanuts, 108
Pear Hazelnut Bars, 84
Raspberry Almond Tarts, 78

**Nuts** *(continued)*

Red Velvet Brownies, 10
Rocky Road Crispy Treats, 116
Santa's Favorite Brownies, 146

# O

Oatmeal Date Bars, 6
Oatmeal S'mores Cookies, 66

**Oats**

Basic Oatmeal Dough, 149
Chocolate 'n' Oat Bars, 61
Chocolate and Oat Toffee Bars, 12
Chocolate Oat Shortbread, 69
Cobbled Fruit Bars, 87
Dinosaur Egg Cookies, 114
Double Chocolate Coconut Oatmeal Cookies, 58
Double Striped Peanut Butter Oatmeal Cookies, 22
Oatmeal Date Bars, 6
Oatmeal S'mores Cookies, 66
O'Henrietta Bars, 54
Pear Hazelnut Bars, 84

O'Henrietta Bars, 54

**Orange**

Chocolate Swirl Lollipop Cookies, 110
Chocolate-Frosted Lebkuchen, 30
Cran-Orange Oatmeal Bars, 92
Orange Snickerdoodles, 100

Original Nestlé® Toll House® Chocolate Chip Cookies, 72

# P

Parmesan Pine Nut Shortbread, 49
PB&J Cookie Bars, 113

**Peanut Butter**

Chewy Peanut Butter Brownies, 60
Chocolate Peanut Butter Swirls, 121
Double Striped Peanut Butter Oatmeal Cookies, 22
Garbage Pail Cookies, 112
PB&J Cookie Bars, 113
Peanut Butter Crème Blossoms, 65
Peanut Butter Toffee Chewies, 5
Peanut Buttery Frosting, 109
Peanuts, 108

Peanut Buttery Frosting, 109
Peanuts, 108
Pear Hazelnut Bars, 84
Philadelphia® Cheesecake Brownies, 74
Philadelphia® Snowmen Cookies, 141
Piña Colada Cookie Bars, 83
**Pineapple**
 No-Bake Pineapple Marmalade Squares, 97
 Piña Colada Cookie Bars, 83
Pink Peppermint Meringues, 143
Pot of Gold Cookies, 117

# R
Raspberry Almond Tarts, 78
Red Velvet Brownies, 10
**Refrigerated Cookie Dough**
 Caramel-Kissed Pecan Cookies, 14
 Jammy Wedges, 99
 Oatmeal Date Bars, 6
 White Chocolate Shamrocks, 127
Rich Cocoa Crinkle Cookies, 55
Rocky Road Crispy Treats, 116
Royal Icing, 153

# S
**Sandwich Cookies**
 Almond Shortbread Cookies with Chocolate Filling, 56
 Whoppie Pies, 8
Santa's Favorite Brownies, 146
Scottish Shortbread Cookies, 41
**Semisweet Chocolate**
 Aztec Brownies, 38
 Black Forest Bars, 68
 Butterscotch Toffee Gingersnap Squares, 24
 Chocolate 'n' Oat Bars, 61
 Chocolate and Oat Toffee Bars, 12
 Chocolate Chunk Cookies, 26
 Chocolate Hazelnut Wedges, 44
 Chocolate Oat Shortbread, 69
 Chunky Pecan Pie Bars, 134
 Classic Layer Bars, 16
 Cocoa Raisin-Chip Cookies, 53

**Semisweet Chocolate** *(continued)*
 Double Chocolate Cherry Cookies, 80
 Double Chocolate Coconut Oatmeal Cookies, 58
 Double Chocolate Pecan Cookies, 81
 Extra-Chocolatey Brownie Cookies, 70
 Irish Flag Cookies, 51
 Mississippi Mud Bars, 21
 Oatmeal S'mores Cookies, 66
 O'Henrietta Bars, 54
 Original Nestlé® Toll House® Chocolate Chip Cookies, 72
 Rocky Road Crispy Treats, 116
 Spiky Pretzel Balls, 103
 Yellow's Nuts for Nutty Squares, 118
S'more Brownies, 120
Spiky Pretzel Balls, 103
Strawberry & Cream Cheese Fudge Brownies, 98
Super-Lucky Cereal Treats, 128

# T
Tea Cookies, 18
Toffee Topping, 29
Tombstone Brownies, 133

# U
**Unsweetened Chocolate**
 Almond Brownies, 104
 Chocolate Spritz, 75
 Chocolate Swirl Lollipop Cookies, 110
 Chunky Double Chocolate Cookies, 62

# W
**White Chocolate**
 Chunky Double Chocolate Cookies, 62
 Lemon Nut White Chip Cookies, 90
 Mississippi Mud Bars, 21
 Piña Colada Cookie Bars, 83
 White Chocolate Shamrocks, 127
Whoppie Pies, 8

# Y
Yellow's Nuts for Nutty Squares, 118

## VOLUME MEASUREMENTS (dry)

$1/8$ teaspoon = 0.5 mL
$1/4$ teaspoon = 1 mL
$1/2$ teaspoon = 2 mL
$3/4$ teaspoon = 4 mL
1 teaspoon = 5 mL
1 tablespoon = 15 mL
2 tablespoons = 30 mL
$1/4$ cup = 60 mL
$1/3$ cup = 75 mL
$1/2$ cup = 125 mL
$2/3$ cup = 150 mL
$3/4$ cup = 175 mL
1 cup = 250 mL
2 cups = 1 pint = 500 mL
3 cups = 750 mL
4 cups = 1 quart = 1 L

## VOLUME MEASUREMENTS (fluid)

1 fluid ounce (2 tablespoons) = 30 mL
4 fluid ounces ($1/2$ cup) = 125 mL
8 fluid ounces (1 cup) = 250 mL
12 fluid ounces ($1 1/2$ cups) = 375 mL
16 fluid ounces (2 cups) = 500 mL

## WEIGHTS (mass)

$1/2$ ounce = 15 g
1 ounce = 30 g
3 ounces = 90 g
4 ounces = 120 g
8 ounces = 225 g
10 ounces = 285 g
12 ounces = 360 g
16 ounces = 1 pound = 450 g

## DIMENSIONS

$1/16$ inch = 2 mm
$1/8$ inch = 3 mm
$1/4$ inch = 6 mm
$1/2$ inch = 1.5 cm
$3/4$ inch = 2 cm
1 inch = 2.5 cm

## OVEN TEMPERATURES

250°F = 120°C
275°F = 140°C
300°F = 150°C
325°F = 160°C
350°F = 180°C
375°F = 190°C
400°F = 200°C
425°F = 220°C
450°F = 230°C

## BAKING PAN SIZES

| Utensil | Size in Inches/Quarts | Metric Volume | Size in Centimeters |
| --- | --- | --- | --- |
| Baking or Cake Pan (square or rectangular) | $8 \times 8 \times 2$ | 2 L | $20 \times 20 \times 5$ |
| | $9 \times 9 \times 2$ | 2.5 L | $23 \times 23 \times 5$ |
| | $12 \times 8 \times 2$ | 3 L | $30 \times 20 \times 5$ |
| | $13 \times 9 \times 2$ | 3.5 L | $33 \times 23 \times 5$ |
| Loaf Pan | $8 \times 4 \times 3$ | 1.5 L | $20 \times 10 \times 7$ |
| | $9 \times 5 \times 3$ | 2 L | $23 \times 13 \times 7$ |
| Round Layer Cake Pan | $8 \times 1 1/2$ | 1.2 L | $20 \times 4$ |
| | $9 \times 1 1/2$ | 1.5 L | $23 \times 4$ |
| Pie Plate | $8 \times 1 1/4$ | 750 mL | $20 \times 3$ |
| | $9 \times 1 1/4$ | 1 L | $23 \times 3$ |
| Baking Dish or Casserole | 1 quart | 1 L | — |
| | $1 1/2$ quart | 1.5 L | — |
| | 2 quart | 2 L | — |